For all girls who love to make pretty things.

Jane Eayre Fryer

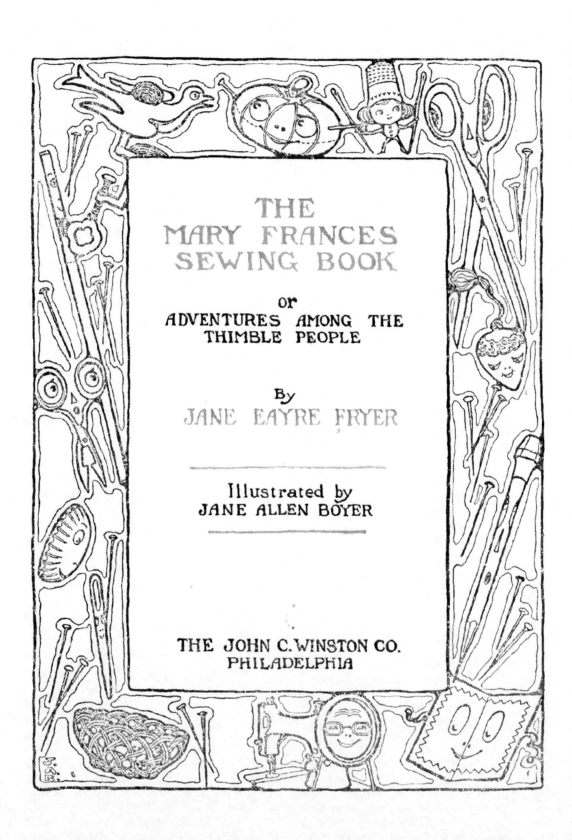

THE MARY FRANCES SEWING BOOK

or
ADVENTURES AMONG THE THIMBLE PEOPLE

By
JANE EAYRE FRYER

Illustrated by
JANE ALLEN BOYER

THE JOHN C. WINSTON CO.
PHILADELPHIA

TT 712
.F8

PREFACE

DEAR GIRLS:

Many of you already know Mary Frances' old friends, the Kitchen People, and have learned to love them. I hope all of you will do so in time.

This book tells the story of Mary Frances' new friends, the Thimble People, who helped her spend a delightful summer vacation at her Grandmother's. It tells how she met Sewing Bird, who was a real Fairy Lady, and the other Thimble People; and how they taught her a lot of fascinating secrets, and finally took her on a long journey to Thimble Land, and brought her back safely, after the most marvelous adventures. Because they proved so helpful and friendly, she wants you to know them, too.

The Thimble People, like the Kitchen People, are peculiar in that they can be of little help to those who dislike them; so that, unless you are prepared to be fond of them, it is best not to seek their acquaintance.

Toward those who show indifference or dislike, they behave in a most contrary manner. For example, Tommy Pin Cushion is a regular porcupine, and bristles right up instinctively at the least inkling of dislike. But if he knows you like him, he will roll over himself to help.

Another thing (and Mary Frances says to be very particular on this point)—if any little girl, who really wishes to learn to sew, will follow the lessons exactly as given by the Thimble People, she can hardly fail to win the Needle-of-Don't-Have-to-Try for her very own.

In the hope that all will achieve this much-to-be-desired end, this record of Mary Frances' new adventures is sent out to the girls of America with the best wishes of

THE AUTHOR.

MERCHANTVILLE, N. J.

CONTENTS

[vii]

LIST OF PATTERNS

INSTRUCTIONS

[xi]

Little Marie has
lost her clothes
And can't tell where
to find them;
Let them alone,
and they'll come
home
With all their
buttons behind
them.

THIMBLE PEOPLE

Sewing **B**ird.

Mr. **S**ilver **T**himble.

Mr. **E**mery **B**ag.

Tommy (Tomato) **P**in **C**ushion.

Scissors **S**hears.

Pen **C**il.

Needle **B**ook.

BodKin.

MaChine.

Work Basket.

Bees Wax.

Yard Stick.

Common Ordinary Pin.

Buttonhole Scissors.
Needle-of-Don't Have-to-Try

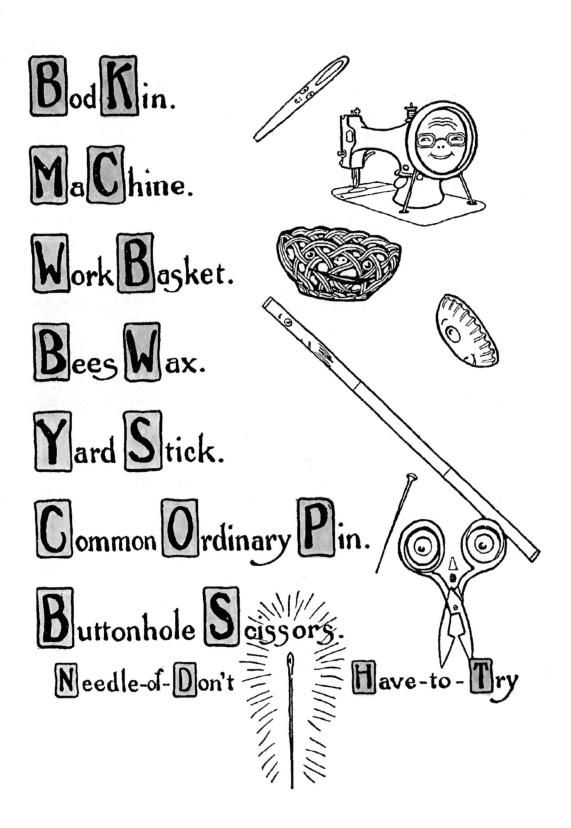

CHAPTER I
SEWING BIRD

"CHEER—UP!" sang a sweet little voice.

Mary Frances looked at the canary; but Dick was very busily preening his feathers, and Dick seldom sang.

"Cheer up!" gurgled again the sweet bird voice.

Mary Frances was certain this time that it was not Dick.

Maybe it was a bird outside!

She looked out of the sewing-room window. No, not a single feather was in sight. All the birds were doubtless in their little nests, or hiding close in the barn to keep themselves warm in such a rain.

"Dick!" said Mary Frances, "Dick, did you speak?"

Dick only ducked his head again for a seed, and snapped off the shell with his strong little bill.

"Peep! Peep! Peep!" sang a bird's voice, as though inviting Mary Frances to a game.

"I'll play 'Hide and Seek,'" thought the little girl.

[17]

"Where are you, Birdie?" she asked aloud; and, throwing Angie on the rocking chair, began to search.

Another soft little "Peep!" drew her near her grandmother's work-basket.

"Why!" she cried, "I could easily believe the voice comes from Grandma's basket!"

"Peep! Peep! Peep! Peep!" the bird voice answered excitedly, as Mary Frances leaned over.

"Why! Why! Why!" she exclaimed.   "If it isn't—if it isn't Grandma's Sewing Bird! You dear little thing! Can you talk, too?" lifting her out. "I never thought of you!"

Peep!
Peep!
Peep!

"Set me up
   Upon the table,
 Then I'll sing
   As I am able,
Chir! Chir!
   Chirp! Chirp!"

answered Sewing Bird.

Mary Frances carried her over to the sewing table and fastened her carefully to the edge, just as she had seen her grandmother do.

Throwing Angie in the rocking chair.

The other Thimble People kept perfectly still, wondering what would happen next.

"Do you know—you remind me of the Kitchen Folks, Birdie," said the little girl.

> "The Kitchen Folks! The Kitchen Folks!
> Of all the joyous, joyous jokes!
> The Thimble People's nearest kin—
> Best friends we are—have always been,"

sang the little bird.

"The Thimble People!" exclaimed Mary Frances; "why, who are they? Are there many Thimble People? And what relation are they to the Kitchen People? Will you tell me all about them? And will they be my little friends?"

> "Tut! Tut!
> So many questions, little maid,
> I cannot answer, I'm afraid—
> But I can say, without a joke,
> Your friends will be the Thimble Folk."

"The Thimble People!"

Sang the little bird

"Oh, I'm so glad! My, I wouldn't have missed knowing them for anything.   Why, I feel as though I've known you for—for—ages!"

"I was so afraid
        You wouldn't find me!
And then, of course,
        You couldn't mind me,
                Chirp!"

Except maybe a mouse

"Oh," said Mary Frances, "wouldn't that have been dreadful!   I was so lonely and dreary that I almost wanted to go home instead of staying here at Grandma's."

"Are you alone
        In the house,
Except maybe a mouse?
        Cheerp!"

asked Sewing Bird.

"No," said Mary Frances, "Katie's in the kitchen, —but she's very busy, and won't bother with me, and my Grandma is out this afternoon, calling on some old ladies."

"Oh, you poor
    Little lonely girl!
It sets my head
    In quite a whirl;
Let me sit here
    On this table,
And comfort you
    As I am able."

"Well, you see, Sewing Bird," began Mary Frances gratefully, "Mother is never very strong, and Father had to go to California on business; and he thought wouldn't it be nice to take Mother with him. So I'm here at my dear Grandma's for the long summer vacation; and brother Billy is camping with the Boy Scouts; Billy is a first-class scout, you know."

"Billy is a first-class scout"

"Yes," said Sewing Bird, pretending to look wise, "they have them in Thimble Land."

"Have what?" asked Mary Frances.

"Why, Boy Scouts, of course—in Thimble Land!"

"Thimble Land!" said Mary Frances; "my, that must be where the Thimble People come from! Where is it?"

Pretending to look wise

"A long way there—
Perhaps you'll go
Some day, if you will
Learn to know
That what we teach
Is sew! sew! sew!"

"So! So! *So!?*" asked Mary Frances, looking puzzled, "What's so?"

"Sew! Sew! Sew!" sang Sewing Bird, looking sharply at her with bright little eyes.

"Sew! Sew! Sew! Sew! Sew! Sew! Sew!"

"Sew!"

"Sew! Sew!" she fairly shrieked.

"Yes," said Mary Frances wondering at her excitement, "of course it's so."

"I mean sew
With a thimble;
I mean sew
And be nimble,"

sang Sewing Bird.

Mary Frances, looking puzzled

"Oh, ho," laughed Mary Frances. "You mean *sew!* How lovely! If I only knew how to really, truly sew! I do, just a little."

> "If you'd like to learn to sew;
> To baste and bind; tie a bow;
> Dress a dolly, head to toe,
> We can teach you how—"

"Can you, really? Really and truly?" cried Mary Frances. "How perfectly dear! Oh, please do, please begin! Angie, poor child, needs so many clothes. When she went to the Tea Party, she spilled cocoa all over herself, and it spoiled all her lovely, lovely dress. It has always grieved me since. She's so tattered and forlorn. Will you teach me how to sew?"

> "I will most gladly; and quite true,
> I'll tell you what you'd better do—
> Get your Grandma every day
> To let you have this room for play."

"Oh, yes, we'll have the sewing-room for a play-room, Sewing Bird; and you give me lessons! Must

"Dress a dolly, head to toe."

"I will most gladly"

they be secret—like the Kitchen People's lessons? And can you teach me? Oh, how happy I am! I wonder if I can surprise my dear mother. Can I learn to sew for my dolly this vacation?"

"A pinafore"

"Why, certainly, dear little Miss,
You can learn to make all this:
A pin-a-fore, some under-clothes,
A little 'kerchief for her nose;
Kimono, bloomers, little cap,
A nightie for her little nap;
A dress for morn, for afternoon,
A dress for parties, not too soon;
A little cape, a little bonnet—
Perhaps with roses fastened on it;—
A nice warm coat to keep from chill,
A dainty sack, in case she's ill:
All this and more we'll gladly teach,
If you will do and follow each—

will you?"

"I will," laughed Mary Frances, "but each what?"

"Some underclothes"

"Each little lesson, one by one,
　　Then, after each hard stitch is done,
　　Remember—'patience brings reward!' "

"What's 'patience'?" asked the little girl.

"Why, 'patience'? Patience is Mary Frances' middle name—Mary P. Frances,—see?"

"My, isn't that a nice name! Mary Patience Frances. And what's 'reward'?" laughed the little girl.

"'Reward'? Reward," said Sewing Bird, "is Angie all dressed up in the things we'll make."

"Oh, I'd love to begin at once—can't we?"

Sewing Bird gaily nodded her bright, shiny little head.

"Goody! Goody! Won't Mother be surprised?" said Mary Frances. "I'll run and get my little work-basket that Grandma gave me."

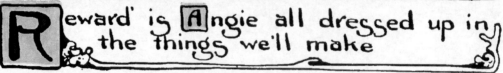

'Reward' is Angie all dressed up in the things we'll make

CHAPTER II

SEWING BIRD BEGINS TO TEACH

THEN Sewing Bird began:

"Little fingers, thin and nimble,
Fit to one, a little thimble;
Right hand—finger, number two—
Put the hat on,—that will do."

Mary Frances put her thimble on the second finger of her right hand.

"I knew that much, Sewing Bird," she laughed.

"What else do you know,
If that much is so?
Chur! Chur! Chur!"

sang Sewing Bird, hopping up and down on one leg.

"Why, I know how to thread my needle," said Mary Frances, to whom the talking of Sewing Bird seemed just as natural as the talking of Tea Kettle and the other Kitchen People.

[26]

Sang Sewing Bird, hopping up and down

"I know, too, that you should put the end of the thread broken off next the spool through the eye of the needle, so that it will not kink."

"Very good,
And very true;—
What in your basket,
Pray, have you?"

asked Sewing Bird.

Then Mary Frances answered, "These are the articles needed, my Grandma said,

To
thread
a needle

1.—To Outfit a Work Basket

1. Spools of cotton, white, Nos. 36, 40, 50, 60, 70, 80; also one of red, No. 50. One spool of basting cotton.

2. One little strawberry emery bag to brighten and sharpen needles.

3. Pins.

4. A piece of beeswax.

5. A tape measure.

6. A pair of scissors.

7. A paper of ground-down needles, Nos. 5's—10's.

8. Some unbleached muslin.

9. Thimble.

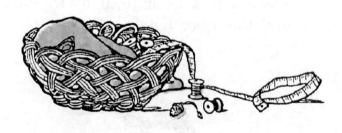

To Outfit a Work Basket

and, oh, look! here is a large piece of Java canvas, and a package of blunt tapestry or zephyr needles, No. 19, and some red D. M. C. working cotton, No. 8, that Grandma put in here yesterday."

"Good," sang Sewing Bird,

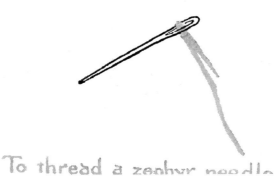

"Oh, that is fine!
Is fine, indeed!
The zephyr needle
Is what we'll need."

"Oh," laughed Mary Frances, "I can thread that—you turn the thread over the needle, double, because a fuzzy end would not go through even this long eye.   Then hold it tight between the thumb and finger, and push the needle over the double thread— this way.   Mother taught me that."

Zephyr
needles
and
working
cotton.

"Needles and pins! Needles and pins!
This is where your lesson begins!
Now, thread your needle,
And knot your thread;
If you know how—
Please do as I've said."

To thread a zephyr needle.

"Yes," laughed Mary Frances. "I know how to knot my thread; I'll show you, after I get this needle threaded—now!

2.—MAKING A KNOT

1. I wind the thread around the tip of the first finger of my left hand.

2. I press it with my thumb and roll the thread downward to the tip end of my finger—so!

3. Then I bring the second finger over the thread on the thumb.

4. Then draw the thread tight with the right hand as I hold it."

"Good! You'll easily
Learn to sew!
How many stitches
Do you know?"

"Let me see," pondered Mary Frances; "there are basting, and running, and hemming!"

"Good!" exclaimed Sewing Bird, in a very nearly human voice, but much more musical and softer. "Good! Now I'll name over all the principal stitches:

"Good!" exclaimed Sewing Bird

Even and uneven basting	Overhanding
Running	Catch-stitching
Back-stitching	Button-hole stitch
Half back-stitching	Darning
Overcasting	Blanket stitch

"My," said Mary Frances. "I had no idea there were that many! I wonder—will I ever learn them all?"

"Oh, yes!" Sewing Bird assured her, "if you come for a lesson whenever you can."

"Indeed I will!" said Mary Frances, "and how I'll thank you, dear little birdie."

Just then the door opened.

"My dear little girl," said Grandma, "how are you? What a dull day!"

"Are you home already, Grandma?" asked Mary Frances. "I had no idea it was time for you to come."

"Ah, my dear, you've not been lonely," said Grandma—then discovering Sewing Bird on the table, "You've been playing with my old-fashioned sewing bird, I see. Many a year this pretty little beak has held Grandma's long seams and hems while she sewed them."

"My dear little girl," said Grandma.

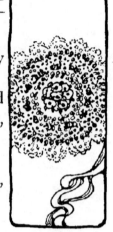

"I think she's lovely!" exclaimed Mary Frances.

"I love her, too, dear," said Grandma, a far-away look coming in her eyes.

"The first time she ever helped me," she added softly, "was with my wedding dress.   Yes, I love her, too, dear."

"Peep!" said a little bird voice.

"Dick," said Grandma, shaking her finger, "Dick, you surely aren't jealous of the little sewing bird!"

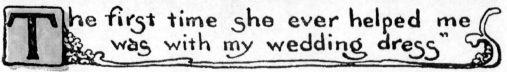

"The first time she ever helped me was with my wedding dress"

CHAPTER III

THE LONG AND SHORT OF BASTING

"Good bye, dear."

"GOOD-BYE, dear," said Grandma, taking leave of Mary Frances a day or two later. "You may play in the garden while I'm gone, if you want to."

"I think I'll stay in, Grandma, if you don't mind," answered Mary Frances, not quite daring to mention her sewing lessons, "I have a sort of an engagement."

"Well! Well!" laughed Grandma, "so grown up already? You have been out every day lately—I think perhaps you'll like to play in the sewing-room."

"I hope you'll have a lovely time, Nanny," said Mary Frances as her grandma closed the door.

"I wonder if Sewing Bird will be ready for the lesson," she thought as she skipped up the stairs to the sewing-room.

"Sewing Bird! Sewing Bird!" she whispered.

[32]

"I hope you'll have a lovely time"

> "Oh, that's the call
> I love to hear;
> I'm always ready—
> Never fear!"

came the sweet singing voice of Sewing Bird.

Mary Frances was delighted.

"I'm so glad you remembered, dear little bird," said she. "Where are you?"

> "Taking a rest,
> In my dear little nest.
> Chur! Chur!"

came the answer.

"Taking a rest in my dear little nest"

"Of course,—the basket's your nest," laughed Mary Frances, carrying Sewing Bird to her place on the table.

"I asked Grandma if I could have the sewing-room for my play-room, and she said, 'Certainly, my dear, you may—anything to keep you happy!'"

"Twitter, twitter, twitter, twit," sang Sewing Bird —and somehow Mary Frances knew she meant, "I'm so happy, too."

"Twitter, twitter, twitter, twit"

"I love to sit
      And sing and sing—
But lesson time
      Is on the wing:
Miss Never-Try
      Never can do;
Miss Never-Begin
      Never gets thru."

*I love
    to sit
And sing
and sing*

"Oh, dear me! Sewing Bird, I want to begin right away," said Mary Frances. "I hope to get so much done!"

"Well," said Sewing Bird, "we will begin at once with that pretty canvas and Turkey-red working cotton (D. M. C. No. 8). You may cut some pieces of canvas seven inches long and one and one-half inches wide. Work on the sewing table—that will be easier."

"Oh, I know," guessed Mary Frances, "the Java canvas is to learn the stitches on."

"Yes," said Sewing Bird, "you use one of these pieces for each new stitch; the regular open spaces in the canvas will help us so much."

"My needle's all ready from the last lesson," said

"I want to begin right-away"

Mary Frances, holding up her threaded needle, "and my thread is knotted."

> "Little Miss! little Miss!
> Not so long a thread!
> Measure it only
> From your hand to your head."

"Oh," said Mary Frances, breaking off some thread. "Thank you, I didn't know that. I suppose it is easier to use only an arm's length of thread."

"Yes," said Sewing Bird. "Now, it would be well to open the skein of cotton."

Mary Frances did so.

"Next clip both ends through—and you will have several threads of the same length."

"That's so much easier," said Mary Frances, "than cutting it each time."

"Now, for a new kind of puzzle," said Sewing Bird. "Take one piece of canvas already cut. For convenience we will call the regular open spaces in the canvas, 'holes.'"

"Yes," said Mary Frances. "I understand, dear Sewing Bird; but please tell me the puzzle."

"Now, for a new kind of puzzle"

"A puzzle then it soon shall be,
  A puzzle which ne'er puzzled me,
  A puzzle which I'll let you see—
Its name is

3.—EVEN BASTING (ON CANVAS)

Cut canvas 7 inches by 1½ inches.

1. Thread needle and knot thread.
2. Count five holes down from upper right hand end of canvas and four holes to the left.
3. Put needle in this hole, pointing downward.
4. Push needle toward the left under two threads, upward through second hole; pull through.
5. Now, again, over two threads under two threads; pull through.
6. Finish the row. Fasten thread by taking two stitches over each other in the same holes at the end. Cut off the thread.

"A puzzle which I'll let you see."

"That's not much of a puzzle," thought Mary Frances, sewing carefully.

"Why is it called Even Basting?" asked Sewing Bird.

"Because the stitches are of the same length," said Mary Frances.

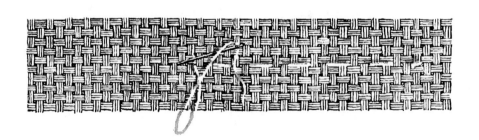

Even Basting

"So wise you are—
  Soon you will be
Quite a little bit
  Too wise for me,"

sang Sewing Bird.

"Ho, ho!" laughed Mary Frances.

"You may wonder why the knot and the finishing threads are on the right side," continued Sewing Bird.

"Oh, I know why," exclaimed Mary Frances. "Because basting stitches are used only to hold the work in place until it is really sewed, then they are easily pulled out if the knot and end are on the right side."

"Oh, I know why."

"Bless my feathers,
  And bless my eye!
Soon you'll know
  As much as I!"

This pleased Mary Frances very much; but she said, "I don't know—for I have no idea what comes next, my dear little teacher."

"Soon you'll know

"Oh, dear me!
Our time we're wasting,
The next stitch is—

4.—UNEVEN BASTING (ON CANVAS)

1. Commence as in Even Basting.
2. Point needle downward, and bring it up through next hole.
3. Count three holes, put needle in downward and bring up next hole—'under one thread, over three' to end of the row.
4. Finish as in Even Basting.

"That wasn't very hard," said Mary Frances, holding up the canvas for Sewing Bird to see.
Then sang Sewing Bird:

"That's all for to-day,—
Put things away;
And, now, little lady,
Good-day, good-day!"

As Mary Frances went down the stairs, she caught the sound of her name. Her grandmother was talking.
"That's a wonderful child," she was saying. "She's

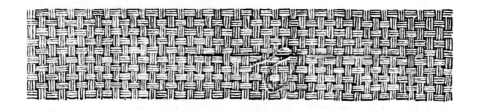

Uneven Basting

no bother at all. She spends hours in the sewing-room, playing with her dolls, just as happy as can be!"

"Dear Nanny!" thought Mary Frances, "I wish I could explain about everything—maybe the Thimble People will let me some day."

Next clip both ends through — and you will have threads of the same length

CHAPTER IV

SEWING BIRD'S SECRET

MARY FRANCES held up her canvas at the beginning of the next lesson, saying:

"Now, I know which of these stitches is which; and I believe I am ready to learn the next, my little teacher!"

"The next," said Sewing Bird, "is

5.—RUNNING STITCH ON CANVAS

'Ouch! That hurts my fingers

1. From under side of canvas, point needle upward, bringing knot on wrong side.

2. Point needle downward through next hole, and upward through next. Pull through.

3. Finish row, by taking several in-and-out stitches on the needle, then pulling through.

4. Turn to wrong side, and fasten by taking three stitches in same hole—this is the 'in-and-out-the-windows' stitch."

"Ouch!" cried Mary Frances. "That hurts my fingers."

"Of course, that is why we have thimbles. Be

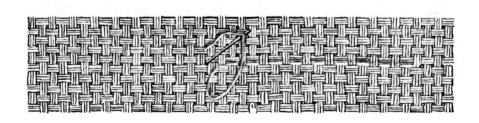

sure to use the knighted soldier finger,—and push the needle with its thimble cap," said Sewing Bird.

"This way?" asked Mary Frances, holding up her little hand.

Then Sewing Bird answered with bright eyes sparkling,

> "Exactly right,
>   And quite bewitching;
> And needed much
>   In learning

6.—Stitching (on Canvas)

(Also called Back-stitching)

1. Enter needle into canvas as for Running.
2. Take one running stitch, bringing needle out on right side.
3. Point needle downward through the hole to the right of the one where the working cotton came out.
4. Push needle under two threads: pull through.
5. Repeat to end of row.
6. Fasten as in running stitch.

"Is that well done?" asked Mary Frances, holding up her first two stitches.

"Exactly
right,
And quite
bewitching

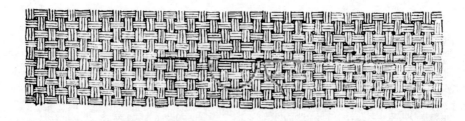

Stitching

"Oh, my, no!" said Sewing Bird. "You've gotten the thread all twisted. Please unthread your needle and take out the work. Then try once more."

"Dear me!" sighed Mary Frances, "one can't be perfect before one learns!"

"Try! Try again!" sang Sewing Bird, flapping her wings,

"Dear me!" sighed Mary Frances

"It is the Thimble People's pride
That they have ever, always, tried:
Whenever they fail,—this is no tale,
As you can easily guess,—
They twist the failure round about,
They twist and turn it inside out;
Then drop it down a big, black hole,
Discovered in back of the North Pole,—
And up it jumps—Success!"

"My, I wish my failures would do that! Maybe they will," mused Mary Frances, finishing the row of stitching very carefully. "Oh, there comes Grandma up the street!"

"Try! Try again!"

"Our lesson is
     Now at an end,—
That's all to-day,
     My little friend,"

just then sang Sewing Bird.

"I forgot to ask," said Mary Frances, "May I show Grandma, or tell her about—about our lessons?"

"That I already
     Should have shown;
I cannot sing
     Where people grown
Can hear: if they hear now
     Or even ever,
I may become
     A Never-Never!"

"Our
  lesson is
Now at
  an end"

"Oh, ho," smiled Mary Frances, softly smoothing the little bird. "I'm so glad I haven't told. I am certainly glad, dear little Teacher Bird—I don't want you to be a Never-Never,—whatever that is."

"Oh, ho! I'm so glad I haven't told"

"A secret let
    Our secret be—
Too much for one,
Enough for two,
And not enough
    For three,"

sang Sewing Bird wisely.   Suddenly—

"Say no more,
    Oh, say no more!
I hear your Grandma
    At the door!"

fluttered the little bird; and Mary Frances quickly
put away her work.

Grandma smiled when she saw Sewing Bird on the
table.

"How you love my little helpful bird, don't you,
dear?" she asked.

"I love her with all my heart," said Mary Frances.

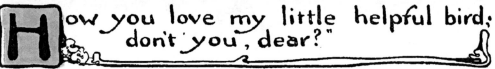

How you love my little helpful bird, don't you, dear?"

CHAPTER V

SEWING BIRD TEASES DICK CANARY

MARY FRANCES heard this through the sewing room door:

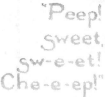

> "Great kind of bird,
>   Upon my word!
>   Who cannot do a thing
>   But sing and eat,
>   And then sing sweet,
>   And then again sing-sing."

"Peep! Sweet, sw-e-et! Che-e-ep!" sang Dick Canary.

> "Of course, you have a pretty voice;
>   Of course, you love to make a noise—
>   If this rhyme sounds a bit contrary,
>   It's good enough for a canary;
>   But, Dick, what I'd really like to know,
>   Is this: why don't you learn to sew?"

[45]

Then Mary Frances stepped in.

"Oh, Sewing Bird," she said, "I didn't think you could be such a tease."

"Good afternoon!
   'Tease,' did you say?
  I wasn't teasing—
   It was only play:
  I thought perhaps that pretty bird
  Would listen to a little word,
  And hold some sewing for his Miss—
  The way I can; See, Dick—like this!"

And hold some sewing for his Miss

holding up a piece of goods in her glistening beak.

"Oh, no," laughed Mary Frances. "I fear Dick would never be able to understand such a useful use of his bill—he's no tailor-bird!"

"Of course, it
   Truly must be so—
  He certainly could
   Not learn to sew;

I see that he
Is surely meant,
Only to be
An ornament,"

sang Sewing Bird. "But our next lesson—is your
canvas ready, child? Yes? This time I'm going to
count by threads instead of holes, when I give directions
for

7.—HALF BACK STITCHING ON CANVAS

1. Commence as in Stitching.
2. One running stitch, under two threads.
3. Point needle downward through hole to the right of hole
from which the cotton hangs; under three threads: pull through.
4. Repeat to end of row. Fasten."

"There!" said Mary Frances, finishing the row.
"That seems like 'two steps backward and one forward,' or rather, 'two forward and one backward.'"

"That's about the way it is!" said Sewing Bird.
"But half back-stitching and back-stitching are both
very strong stitches. Why, when your grandma was
little, she stitched all seams by hand. Sewing machines
were a great cu-cur—"

"Curiosity," smiled Mary Frances

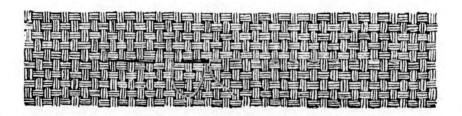

Half back stitching

"Peep—peep," giggled Dick Canary.

"Thank you, Miss Mary Frances," said Sewing Bird,

"Perhaps that little yellow bird
Thought I didn't know the word;
It's funny that it seems a joke
When anybody stops to choke—
Ahem! Ahem! Ahem! Ahack!
Pat-me-on-the-back!
Pat-me-on-the-back! Quick!"

"Better?" asked Mary Frances, smiling to herself, and patting the little bird's back.

After a minute she said, "Excuse me, but is—the next stitch—is the next stitch a fancy one?"

"It is!" said Sewing Bird, "and is called

"Peep—peep"

8.—CATCH STITCHING ON CANVAS

1. At left hand end of canvas, count four holes down and four to the right.

2. From under side, point needle upward: pull through.

3. Count three holes down and three to the right. Point needle down and under this, one hole to the left: pull through.

4. Count four holes to the right of first stitch. Point needle down through next hole to the left: pull through.

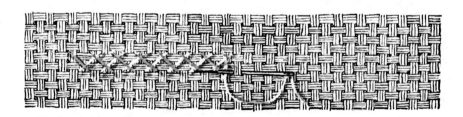

Catch Stitching

"Is that right?" asked Mary Frances.

"My, no," said Sewing Bird.   "That is all wrong. Hold the work here near my beak.   There, let the thread hang this way:

"Now, pull it through.   In taking the next stitch, let the thread hang this way:

"There, that is better."

"Oh, I see, now," said Mary Frances.   "Isn't that a beautiful stitch!"

"Yes," said Sewing Bird,—then, suddenly.

"Beware! Beware!
Beware! Beware!
I hear your Grandma
On the stair—
    Good-bye!"

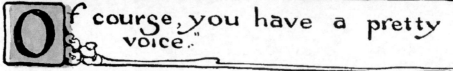

Of course, you have a pretty voice."

CHAPTER VI

THE STITCH GRANDMA LEARNED

MARY FRANCES stopped on the stairs to listen.

"Surely," she thought, "Sewing Bird is talking with some one. I wonder if it's one of the Thimble People. Oh, I do hope so!" and, as she tripped into the sewing-room, she asked,

"Oh, Sewing Bird, what's that I heard as I came up the stair? It really doesn't matter much—for Grandma wouldn't care."

"What's that I heard?"

> "I cannot tell you what you heard,
>   My dearest little Miss;
> But listen to a wisdom-word,
>   For I can tell you this:
> If many times you make up rhymes,
>   You may become a little bird,"

sang Sewing Bird.

"Oh," laughed Mary Frances. "Caught myself

"I cannot tell you what you heard.

making a rhyme;—but I don't want to become a little birdie, even though they are so dear,—besides, I don't have wings."

"No," said Sewing Bird. "I don't suppose you do want to be a birdie—for many reasons;—but the most important must be that little birds do not have hands!"

"Hands are so wonderful!" said Mary Frances, "they can do so many things. They are pincers, hammers, wedges, and yet they can do the most dainty, delicate work."

"Yes," said Sewing Bird, "they come in handy!"

"Oh, ho, hee-hee!" laughed Mary Frances.

"Chirp, chirp!" twittered Dick Canary.

"Hands are so wonderful!"

> "Oh, Dick! oh, Dick!
> What lots of fun!
> Do you pretend
> To see a pun?"

asked Sewing Bird. "But now to learn

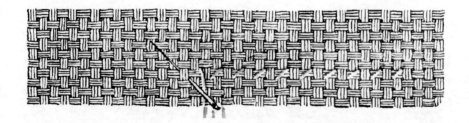

9.—OVERHANDING ON CANVAS

1. Count six holes down and four from right hand end. Put needle in from under side: pull through.

2. Count one hole to the left. Find the hole above it. Point needle downward through the upper hole—bring it up to right side through the under hole.

3. Finish row and fasten thread on wrong side, by running thread through the last few stitches.

10.—OVERCASTING ON CANVAS

1. Count one hole from top of canvas and two in from end.

2. Commence as for Overhanding.

3. Bring needle out two holes to the left of first stitch.

4. Fasten as in Overhanding.

Overcasting stitch is used to finish raw edges of material to keep from fraying.

Over-handing

"The next stitch is the first stitch your grandmother learned to make," said Sewing Bird. "Her little fingers got so tired and sore trying to make tiny little bits of stitches on muslin, that you may be glad you are to learn on canvas."

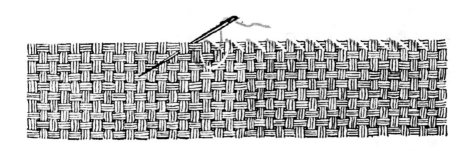

Overcasting

11.—HEMMING STITCH ON CANVAS

1. Six rows from top—four over to left. Needle up from wrong side: pull through.

2. On row of holes below, one hole to left, point needle down, bring it up in first row of holes, two holes to the left of first stitch.

3. Hood canvas over the first finger. Finish row.

4. Fasten as in Overcasting.

"Is that all there is to hemming?" asked Mary Frances happily.

"No, little Miss, that is just a 'first beginning,' as my grandmother used to say. Some day I hope you will make hemming stitches so small that they will scarcely show—on a dolly's apron."

"Oh, how perfectly lovely!" cried Mary Frances. "I can scarcely wait! Will it be long?"

"That all depends, my little friend—"

"Upon me," said Mary Frances. "I'll work very in-dus-tri-ous-ly, dear little teacher."

But the most important must be that little birds do not have hands

CHAPTER VII

BLANKET STITCH AND ITS SISTER

"NOW, Sewing Bird," began Mary Frances the next lesson afternoon, "let's not talk any, but—"

"Let us get right to our lesson," said Sewing Bird, "which is an edge-finishing stitch, named

"Let us get to our lesson"

12.—BLANKET STITCH

1. At left hand end of canvas four holes down and four to right, from under side bring needle to right side.

2. Hold thread under thumb. One hole to the right, point needle down, bringing it up in hole two threads below: pull through. Finish row.

3. Fasten as in Overcasting.

4. Repeat this on lower edge of canvas.

"Good!" she said, as Mary Frances finished following the directions, "Now, for a stitch many grown women do not know how to make—a beautiful stitch:

[54]

13.—BUTTONHOLE STITCH ON CANVAS

1. Five holes down—four from left hand end, from wrong side, bring needle to right side.

2. Through hole below this, point needle down, and up through the one from which the thread hangs. Do not pull through.

3. Take hold of the two threads in the eye of the needle, bring them toward you around under the point of the needle. Let them rest there.

4. Pull needle through.

5. With left thumb on the stitch, pull the thread with the right hand tightly down to the edge of the canvas.

6. Repeat to end of row.

"Oh, look! dear Sewing Bird," cried Mary Frances, holding up her work, "I really do believe that is the way Mother makes a buttonhole! She said she would show me how to do it very soon. How glad I am I know that stitch!"

"Yes," said Sewing Bird. "Won't she be surprised! You know eleven stitches now."

"Why, so I do!" exclaimed Mary Frances, counting her little samplers of work.

"Now," said Sewing Bird," will you please cut a piece of canvas eight inches long and four and one-half

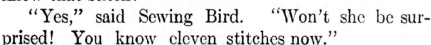

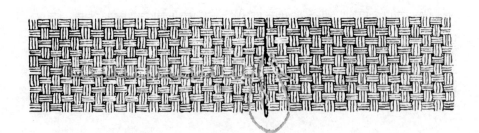

Buttonhole Stitch

inches wide, and make a sampler of all the stitches you know. Will you write down the directions?"

"Yes," said Mary Frances, getting pencil and paper. Then Sewing Bird began:

14.—CANVAS SAMPLER

1. Begin six rows down, and five rows from right hand end with a row of Uneven Basting.

2. A row each of even basting; Running Stitch; Stitching; Catch Stitching; Buttonhole Stitching; Hemming,—each two rows apart.

3. A row of Overhanding—five rows below that.

4. Blanket Stitch the upper edge

5. Overcast the two ends.

6. Fold canvas back on row of overhanding at bottom of samples.

"Yes" said Mary Frances

"Will you bring the pretty sampler, finished, for the next lesson?" asked Sewing Bird.

"I will—so gladly!" said Mary Frances.

> "But there's one stitch more,
>   There's one stitch more!
> If it hadn't been so cross,
>   I'd have shown it before,"

added Sewing Bird.

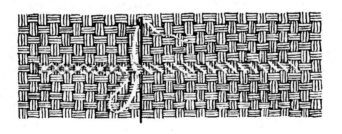

Cross Stitching

15.—CROSS STITCHING

1. Cut a canvas piece, five inches long and three inches wide.

2. At the right hand end from under side, two holes from the edge, and eight holes down, point needle upward.   Pull through.

3. Point needle downward into hole above the hole to the left of where thread hangs out, and bring it up through the hole directly beneath.

4. Continue across the canvas.

5. Return on same row of stitches in same way, but work from left to right, taking stitches in exactly the same holes as at first.   This will form a cross.   The stitches must all be taken in the same direction.

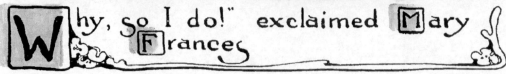

"Why, so I do!" exclaimed Mary Frances

CHAPTER VIII

SEWING BIRD FAIRY LADY

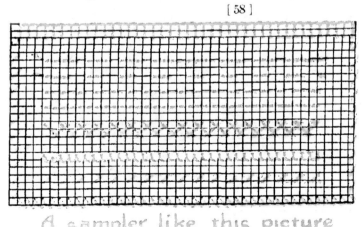

MARY FRANCES worked very hard whenever she could find a minute; and the next lesson day she proudly showed Sewing Bird a sampler like this picture:

> "Oh, de-de-dum-dee! de-de-dee!
> That sampler certainly pleases me.
> You did it alone? Well, I declare!
> What perfect stitches you have there!"

sang the little bird, hopping, fluttering, gurgling, and spreading her wings joyously over Mary Frances' work, very much the way a spring robin careens over an early worm.

Mary Frances was very happy.

"Now, Sewing Bird, my dear teacher, please tell me what I am to learn next?" asked Mary Frances, finishing the row of cross stitching.

A sampler like this picture

"Indeed I will!   Indeed I will!
Just watch a while my little bill;
And I to you will quickly tell,
And you will quickly do, and well,
This lesson coming next."

With these words, the little bird leaned over the edge of the table and stuck her bill into the drawer beneath.   Then she pulled out a long sheet of paper.

'Oh,' gasped Mary Frances, "what is that, dear teacher?"

'That,' said Sewing Bird, shaking her wings, "is a model for you to follow in making,

"Won't it be beautiful!"

15.—GRAND SAMPLER ON CANVAS

Cut a piece of canvas twelve inches by nine inches, and follow as exactly as you can the picture on the next page.

"Won't it be beautiful!" exclaimed Mary Frances, "I'll do it in all the pretty colors—I have almost every shade of mercerized working-cotton here."

"Yes," said Sewing Bird,

She pulled out a long sheet of paper

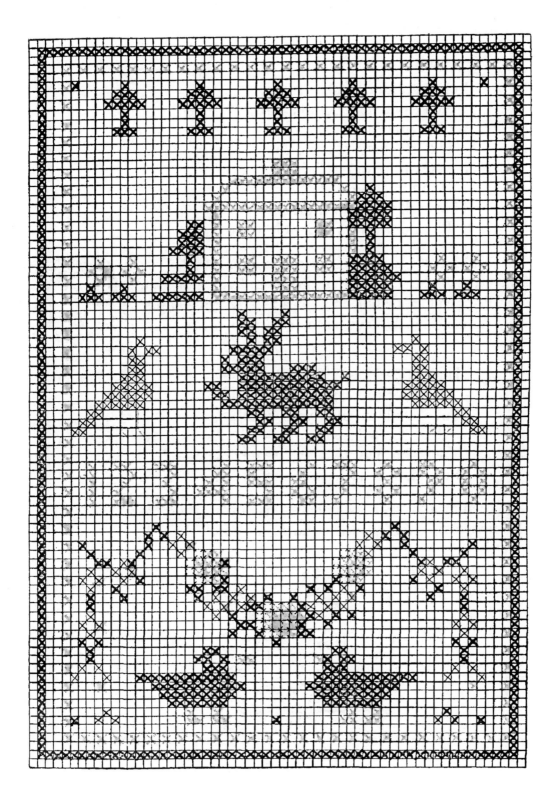

"Your Grandma took a prize
  At Persimmon County Fair,
With a pretty sampler
  Like the picture lying there;
If you work yours aright,
  'Twill be a prettier thing,
That well may win a prize,
  From our merry Thimble King."

"All right!" laughed Mary Frances. "I'll work from time to time on the Grand Sampler. But, Sewing Bird, will you tell me, please—are you—aren't you, a real fairy? You seem so like a fairy 'come true!' "

"Dear little Miss, I'll give you
  A secret to keep.
Put your hand over your eyes,
  And don't dare to peep!
Now, you may take away your hand—
  Behold, a Lady from Thimble Land!"

When
Mary
Frances
opened
her eyes

When Mary Frances opened her eyes, there sat the loveliest, sweetest little fairy lady on the edge

The loveliest, sweetest fairy lady

of the table in place of Sewing Bird;—only Mary Frances noticed her lips looked very much like the bill of a bird.

"Oh, oh, oh, oh, oh!" gasped Mary Frances in surprise. "Oh, really, truly, oh, me! Oh, dear! How perfectly lovely! You lovely—"

"Now, Mary Frances, dear, ready for the lesson," smiled the little lady, in the same flute-like voice as Sewing Bird's.

"Miss Fairy," said Mary Frances, trembling with joy, "I will do my very best,—but, please, what may I call you?"

"Just shut your eyes,
    And not a word;
My name you have
    So often heard;
It's known to
    But a very few,
But I will show
    My name to you—"

When Mary Frances opened her eyes, there sat her grandmother's sewing bird.

"You dear little bird," she exclaimed. "I know now! You are the Fairy!—and I know!—the Fairy's name is Sewing Bird!"

'Just so! Just so! Just so! Just so!" sang Sewing Bird,—

"Now quickly shut your eyes—and then
    The Fairy Lady will come again!"

And again came Fairy Lady.

"Oh," laughed Mary Frances, "dear Sewing Bird Fairy Lady, please wait a minute," and running out of the room, she brought back her doll's rocking chair and put it on the table.

"Please be more comfortable!" she said.

"Thank you very much, dear child!" said Fairy Lady.

"Now, for work! Cut a piece of unbleached muslin, nine inches long and five and one-half inches wide.

"Good!" she exclaimed, as Mary Frances held up the muslin properly cut.

"Pen Cil," the fairy called.

With a bound, a yellow lead pencil which lay on

"Pen Cil," the fairy called

"Thank you very much, dear child"

the machine, sprang over to the table and made a funny little stiff bow to Sewing Bird Fairy Lady, who picked up a big bodkin and, using it as a sceptre, touched him, saying—

"Mark off the muslin as I told you."

To Mary Frances' amazement, Pen Cil marked off the muslin like this:

"You may retire," said Fairy Lady, "Thank you,—and Mary Frances, child, you may sew the muslin very much as you did the Canvas Sampler, with that finer red D. M. C. cotton, No. 12."

"Am I to be forgotten?" came a tinkling sound from Mary Frances' basket, as she started to sew.

"Who is that?" asked Mary Frances peeping over the edge.

"I'm Thimble!" exclaimed a wee little voice, "and the reason I always wear my helmet, is that I want to wield my sword," as Mary Frances lifted him out.

"I beg your Majesty's pardon," said the little fellow turning to Sewing Bird Fairy Lady—"but perhaps Miss Mary Frances doesn't understand that all needles are my swords!"

"He thinks himself so brave a soldier," laughed

Marked off the muslin like this

"Am I to be forgotten?"

Sewing Bird Fairy Lady—"when all the time he is perfectly useless by himself."

"But he is a great help," said Mary Frances. "I don't see how I could sew without him."

"Good!" said Fairy Lady. "But he'll be prouder than ever! That's all for to-day—next lesson we will make something for your dolly to use."

"Oh, how lovely!" exclaimed Mary Frances, finishing her last stitches. "What is it?"

> "Oh, well! oh, well, O!
>   I best not tell, O!
>   But something she can use real well, O!
>   Now for to-day, farewell,
>   Farewell, O!"

And as Mary Frances looked up from her work, there was the empty rocking chair and her grandmothers, sewing bird was sitting on its perch on the table.

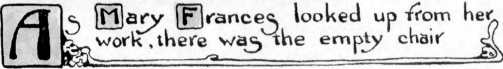

As Mary Frances looked up from her work, there was the empty chair

Chapter IX

Magic and Mystery

"I'M Cross Patch, Cross Patch!
Nobody dares to lift the latch!
I'm Cross Patch, Cross Patch!
Click–ety—clatch!
Cross Patch!"

"Can I talk?"

Mary Frances heard this outside the sewing room door.

"My," she thought, "that sounds like the scissors—I really believe it is!" She peeped in, and this is what she saw:

Scissors Shears was strutting on tip-toe up and down the sewing table, closing up each time to take a step.

"Why," said Mary Frances, slipping in, "can you talk, too?"

"Can I talk?" exclaimed Scissors Shears in a growling voice. "Can I talk? Yes, and walk, too! As if I weren't years older than that Sewing Bird—

"Can you talk?"

Rip 'er up the back! Rip 'er up the back! That conceited thing thinks she knows everything,—why I could tell you all about how to cut out anything. Why, I know all about cutting things out! I can even cut myself!"

Click—click, came his legs together.

"Well, well," laughed Mary Frances. "If that is so, perhaps Sewing Bird will let you explain some things to me."

"It cuts me to the quick to be cut like this," he started again,—then Sewing Bird began to sing,

"If anything you'd like to do,
To prove yourself so very true—
Immediately to work—don't brag!
Cut out

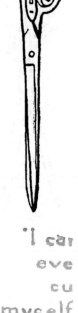

'I car
eve
cu
myself

PATTERN 1.—DOLL'S LAUNDRY BAG

Cut bag twelve inches long, and five inches wide.

"What goods, what goods?" asked Scissors Shears, excitedly.

"Cut it out of that pretty calico on the table," said Sewing Bird.

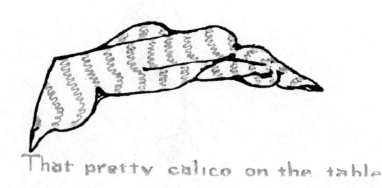

That pretty calico on the table

"Hurrah!" shouted Scissors Shears, and dived into the calico.

"There!" he exclaimed proudly. "Isn't that perfect?"

"That's very even," said Mary Frances gravely, trying to act as though she were an excellent judge.

"What next?" she asked Sewing Bird.

"When you want me otherwise
    Than as a little bird,
Put your hand over your eyes,
    And say this secret word:

        Magic and Mystery,
        Give my wish to me."

Mary Frances did so; and there was Fairy Lady once again in the doll's rocking chair, who smiled and said,

"Whenever you particularly want 'this me' to come, all you have to do is to put your hands over your eyes, and say to yourself quickly,

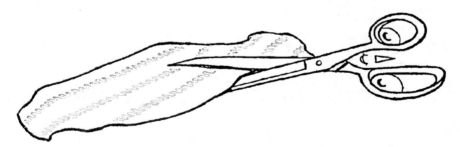

Dived into the calico

agic and Mystery!" exclaimed Mary Frances

> Magic and Mystery,
> Give my wish to me,

and I'll come at once."

"Oh, how lovely!" said Mary Frances.

"And if you want *me* to turn into anything, you say as fast as you can,

> Nimble, nimble,
> Turn my thimble,"

said Thimble, looking up at Mary Frances with a comical smile.

"And if you want *me* to turn into some one else, snap your fingers three times and say, faster yet,

> Scissors-and-Shears,
> Scissors-and-Shears,
> Now change your ears,
> Now change your ears."

"I'll do it now," laughed Mary Frances, and when she said,

"I'll come at once"

"Nimble, nimble,

"Nimble, nimble,
Turn my thimble,"

there sprang up the cutest little soldier, with needles in his hands for swords.

"Salute!" he shouted in a very thin silvery voice, making a military bow to Fairy Lady.

"At your service!" he said, turning to Mary Frances, who was looking on with amazement.

"Are you really my own thimble?" she asked, looking at the second finger of her right hand.

"It's me—I, I mean—I'm he—it, I mean—well, anyhow, I'm Thimble, your Seamstress-ship," he answered, making another bow.

"Well, well," said Mary Frances delightedly, "if you are, you can obey my orders.

"Stand there!" pointing to the left side of Fairy Lady. Then,

At
your
service!"

"Scissors-and-Shears,
Now change your ears,"

she repeated.

"Scissors and Shears.

Click! came the feet of the shears, and before Mary
Frances saw how it happened, there were two long ears
on the handles, looking comically like a rabbit's.

"What long ears you have!" laughed the little
girl.

"The better to hear your directions, your Seamstress-ship," replied Scissors in a rather sharp voice,
clicking his way to the other side of the rocking
chair.

Then Fairy Lady said:

"Dear little Lady Seamstress, we are all from
Thimble Land—we are the Thimble People; there are
many more of us, oh, many more. It is our joy to be
able to help you learn to sew. Thimble and Scissors
Shears and the other Thimble People will come help us
when anything becomes very puzzling or difficult; but
all through these lessons you may call upon *me* at any
time; and I shall do my best to give you happy sewing
lessons."

"Oh, thank you, dear Fairy Lady," exclaimed Mary
Frances. "I am living in Fairyland, and it is real!"

"The way to find Fairyland real," smiled Fairy
Lady, "is to do your very best from day to day, and

There
were two
long ears

to do it happily.   The fairies always help the people who try to do this."

"Oh, pshaw!" exclaimed Scissors Shears in a cutting tone, "what twoddle-doddle!   Even if I don't make fine speeches, I know all about cutting."

"Cut it out!" exclaimed Thimble, raising his sword-needle.

"Slang," began Scissors Shears, crossly flapping his ears back; but Fairy Lady leaned forward in her chair, and, reaching out with her bodkin wand, touched him on the ear, and down he fell flat at her feet.

Pushing him aside, she said, "I can control him when I have my wand.   If he's ever rude, and you want me, say the magic verse I taught you."

"Oh, thank you," said Mary Frances, smiling to herself.

"I guess if I pulled his ears real hard, he'd be good anyhow," she thought, "but I'll not let Sewing Bird know.   All rabbits are controlled by their ears, and I'm sure he looks more like a rabbit than any other animal I can think of."

"Well," smiled Fairy Lady, "we have the dolly's laundry bag all cut out: now, to learn,

"What twoddle-doddle!"

"Cut it out!"

17.—HEMMING ON MUSLIN

1. First learn to turn a hem on paper.
2. Cut the paper seven inches long and three and one-half inches wide.
3. Draw a line one-quarter of an inch from lower edge of paper and turn up and crease along this line.
4. One inch above that, draw a line. Turn up and crease along that line.
5. Follow same directions on muslin. Baste and hem.

"Good!" she nodded, as Mary Frances held up the folded paper. "You remember the hemming stitch on canvas. This is the same kind of stitch; only, as you have already observed, no doubt, it is a very zig-zag stitch, and is taken from the single through the folded part of the goods.

"Wait a minute, I'll mark it to show you," and taking the pencil, she marked the paper as shown on this page.

"Now try it on muslin."

"Oh," exclaimed Mary Frances. "I understand now!"

"Only one thing more," said Fairy Lady, "the way to hide the starting of the thread. You put the

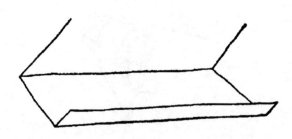

First learn to turn a hem on paper

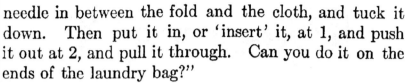

needle in between the fold and the cloth, and tuck it down.   Then put it in, or 'insert' it, at 1, and push it out at 2, and pull it through.   Can you do it on the ends of the laundry bag?"

"Yes, I think I can," said Mary Frances.

"One minute," said Fairy Lady, as Mary Frances started.

"First, you must turn in the edges.   Here is a piece of paper the size of the laundry bag.

"On the longer edge, turn up and crease a quarter of an inch fold as you did in preparing the paper hem. Now, turn the hem on each end as I have already shown you.

"That's it!—and that's all for to-day's lesson. It was a tech-ni-cal lesson," she said.

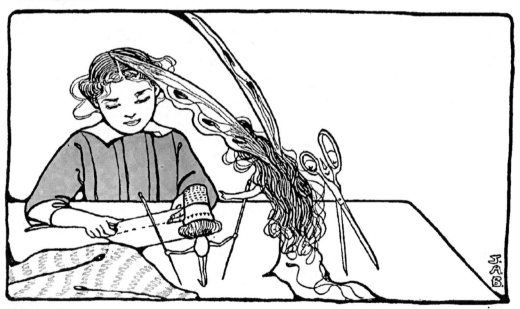

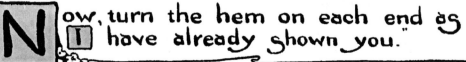

Now, turn the hem on each end as I have already shown you."

CHAPTER X

A DOLL'S LAUNDRY BAG

"NOW, try it on the laundry bag itself," smiled Fairy Lady, who was waiting for Mary Frances next Wednesday.

"That's hard to crease!" exclaimed the little girl, laying the calico down on the table and pressing the fold with her thumb nail.

"Yes," said Fairy Lady. "It is a good idea to pinch it together between the thumb and forefinger, to make the crease."

"Oh, that is much better," said Mary Frances, and she soon had the little bag folded ready for sewing.

"What now?" smiled Fairy Lady.

"I begin to hem," said Mary Frances, flourishing her threaded needle.

"What number cotton are you using?" asked Fairy Lady.

"Number twenty-four," said Mary Frances.

"Ahem," Thimble cleared his throat.

[75]

"Now, try it on the laundry bag"

Pinch it together between thumb and forefinger

"A little too coarse," said Fairy Lady. "I must tell you something about needles and threads:

"There are several different kinds of

18.—NEEDLES AND THREADS

Sharps—long needles.

Betweens—short needles for heavy work.

Ground-downs—medium long. These do not break or bend easily.

There are the long-eyed needles—worsted and darning needles.

Milliner's very long needles.

Bodkins—long thick needles, for carrying tapes and cords.

Open a package of needles No. 5's to 10's. In the middle, you will find needles

No. 5—for coarse work or sewing on buttons.

No. 6—for coarse work.

No. 7—for hemming towels.

No. 8—for stitching.

No. 9—for hemming muslin.

No. 10—for fine work.

Use	Needle	Cotton
For Tucking, Hemming, Running.	No. 9	No. 60, 70 or 80
For Stitching, Overhanding, Over-casting....................	No. 8	No. 50 or 60
Buttonholes....................	No. 7 or 8	No. 36, 40 or 50
Gathering and Basting..........	No. 7 or 8	No. 36 or 40

"Oh," murmured Mary Frances, "I didn't know."

"Of course you didn't, dear little Seamstress," smiled Fairy Lady. "That's why I'm here!"

"Thank you, Fairy Lady," said Mary Frances.

"Now, you may begin work on the laundry bag."

Mary Frances smilingly basted the hems near the edges with even basting stitches, and then began to do the hemming.

Fairy Lady watched her intently all the while.

"There!" Mary Frances suddenly exclaimed. "I've broken my thread. How do I join it?"

"I will show you this once," said Fairy Lady. "You do it in very much the same way as in starting the work," and she taught Mary Frances how to tuck both ends of thread under the hem.

"Thank you, Fairy Lady"

"When you finish, just fasten the thread by taking two or three stitches in the fold. That's a pretty good looking hem for the first real hem on muslin," said Fairy Lady.

"Now, one-quarter of an inch above the hems, put in a row of running stitches,—with once in a while a back-stitch to strengthen it. This is called combination stitch."

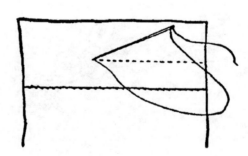

This is called combination stitch

When Mary Frances had done this, she held up the bag, and asked, "What shall I do next?"

"I'll tell you more,
    I'll tell you more,
If you can tell
    What that is for!"

"I know," guessed Mary Frances.   "It's for a casing to hold the drawing strings."

"Oh, to my heart
    That music rings,
For you to guess
    It's 'drawing strings,' "

sang Fairy Lady.

"How could her heart draw strings," asked Scissors Shears of Thimble, in a whisper.

"Hush!" said Silver Thimble, raising his sword-needle.

"Snip!" snapped Scissors Shears.   But Fairy Lady, not noticing, continued the lesson.

"Hush!"
said Silver
Thimble

"What this is for?"

"Do you remember the overhanding stitch on canvas? Yes? Now, those little ends of the bag above the running stitches, are to be overhanded together. You put the needle in straighter, and more toward you—like this." as she placed the needle in position.

"Now fold the two hemmed ends together, the right sides facing each other.

"Baste along the longer edges with even basting. Overhand these edges together.

"You would not always overhand the sides of a bag together,—you could run it, or back-stitch, or combination stitch it; but we want this unusually strong because your dolly will have so many clothes to be stuffed into it. I should say handkerchiefs, because this bag is really a handkerchief bag, or a *little* laundry bag."

"My, how well you have done this side. Let me touch the other side with my bodkin wand—there!" And behold, the other side was overhanded.

"That's lovely, thank you, dear Fairy Lady!" exclaimed Mary Frances, examining the perfectly beautiful stitches. "How did—?"

"Let me touch the other side

And behold the other

"Oh, that was done
In Thimble Land—
Done by the Fairy
Needle Band."

laughed the little lady, well pleased at Mary Frances' delight.

"Now, thread this narrow tape into a bodkin, and run it into the casing, all the way round; then tie the ends together. Now, another piece (they are twelve inches long) in the other end, and tie."

"Oh, if it isn't the dearest little bag I ever saw!" exclaimed Mary Frances, drawing the top together. "Isn't it lovely! Look, Fairy Lady!"

But Fairy Lady had gone, and Sewing Bird sat in her usual place on the table, singing:

"Oh, little Miss, dear little Miss,
There never was a joy like this:
To keep some one from being sad,
To make some dear one very glad.
Oh, little lady—"

Crash!

The Laundry bag

Sewing Bird sat up stiff and hard and metallic.

"Good joke!" giggled Scissors Shears, who had jumped on the floor to scare her.

Mary Frances glanced at Sewing Bird, but the door knob was turning, and she hastily threw her sewing into her basket.

"Bring a piece of white lawn for the next lesson," whispered Sewing Bird, throwing Mary Frances a kiss with the tip of her wing.

The door knob was turning — she threw her sewing into her basket.

CHAPTER XI

MR SILVER THIMBLE AND MR EMERY BAG

"May I have this little piece of lawn?"

"GRANDMA," asked Mary Frances, the next afternoon, "may I have this little piece of white lawn?"

"Why, certainly, dear," said Grandma. "You are such a good child. I am sure I never saw a little girl who was so able to amuse herself."

"My, I wish I could explain about my little friends," thought Mary Frances, but she answered, "I don't get very lonely when you are away, Nanny dear, because I keep busy; and when you are here, we have such fun together!"

"Heigho!" exclaimed Grandma, "I feel really young again!"

. . . .

"Go to sleep! go to sleep!
Baby dear, baby dear, mine.
To and fro, I rock thee deep,

[82]

My arms a cradle for thy sleep;
Close your eyes, and don't you peep,
    Baby dear, baby dear, mine.

"I rock thee deep, but hold thee near,
    Baby dear, Baby dear, mine.
Nothing can harm thee, never fear!
Mother-love is so very queer,
Nothing can make thee but my dear
    Baby—baby mine,"

sang Mary Frances, rocking Angie in her arms.

"My, I'm glad I got that child to sleep before my sewing lesson," she said.

"I hope she'll be quiet all through the afternoon. Every once in a while I've had to take her over to Lottie's to stay. I've put myself under ob-li-ga-tion to Lottie, and I'll have to make something for one of her children—oh, I wonder if I could give her some sewing lessons, the way I did Eleanor cooking lessons.

"How I wish Eleanor were here! I do miss her so!

"I'll tip-toe in to my lesson with this child in my arms, and put her carefully in the big rocking chair,

"I wonder if I could give her lessons"

"Baby—baby mine"

so as to have her near if she cries. Of course, I'm only pretending she's a tiny young thing—because I didn't bring my baby infant doll with me, and this is only Angie. She's really almost three years old; but my, she certainly does love to be 'babied'—and I'd certainly get very lonesome if I didn't do it—with Mother and Father so far away—and Billy in camp!"

The big tears rolled down her cheeks.

"Come, Mary Frances," she said. "I feel like shaking you. When you promised Father so faithfully to be a woman, and your Grandma is such a darling!—Suppose you read Mother's last letter over:

Dear Little Big Mary Frances:

Only twenty times has Mother read over your sweet letter. It was so dear, and brave. I am much better than I was—thanks to such a loving family—and the lovely "aps-mos-spere" here, as you used to say when you were little.

What a beautiful country this is—your "Fatherland" and mine. I want you to see some day the lovely view I am now looking upon: mountains rising high and peeping over this lovely stretch of country to look

Read Mother's last letter

into the Pacific Ocean, which sparkles like that ir-i-des-cent feather in your dear Grandma's bonnet.

Father is calling me to come for a ride, and I must drop a line to my Billy Boy—who is a good Scout, too.

Can you feel this kiss and this hug?   I know you can—for what are miles to us whose love for each other flies through space?

Your loving Mother.

P. S.—*Thank you so much for the picture of Jubey.*

"My, I feel better," said Mary Frances, drying her tears.   "But if it weren't for my sewing lessons, even with Grandma's help, I'd not be a Scout.   Billy is a good Scout:—but now,—for the lesson," and she went to the sewing-room very softly, with Angie asleep in her arms.

With Angie asleep in her arms

"Hee-ha!" she heard through the door, which was a very tiny way open, "that's the time!"

She thought it was the voice of Silver Thimble.

"I don't care," answered a new voice.   "It's too much, to have to clean them all at once."

"Oh, there are only two more.   Come, I'm ready—it is really excellent practice for a soldier!"

"It is really excellent practice"

"Take 'em out, take 'em out, I say!"

Mary Frances feared to make a noise—but she quietly pushed the door open a little wider and saw Silver Thimble on one side of the table, and over on the opposite side, the queerest little fellow.

"Looks like the picture of a porcupine," thought Mary Frances.

"It may be good practice for a soldier," groaned the queer little figure, "but pity the target! Besides, —one at a time, please!"

"Emery Bag, what do you think you were made for? I hope you realize it's your duty to clean all the rust and roughness off these needles as I run them through you, so that the little Miss may sew more easily," lectured Thimble. "No in-sub-or-din-a-tion! Stop and think! You know my family's power,—you know my family's wealth. You realize, I hope, you live in a land named for my aris-to-crat-ic ancestors— Thimble Land!"

"Oh, ancestors go-to-China!" exclaimed Emery Bag. "We live in the present, and I demand—I demand justice. I leave it to anybody if it's fair to have twenty needles stuck into your heart at once!"

"No in-sub-or-din-a-tion!"

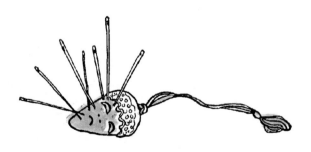

"Take 'em out. I say!"

"The idea of being such a coward!" retorted
Thimble. "Where's your heart of steel you brag of
so often?"

"It's scarcely fair, you know," came a new voice.
"You see, twenty needles at once are really more than
are needed."

"Humph, Tommy Pin Cushion," answered Silver
Thimble. "What you sticking your 'pinion in for?
It's a wonder Sewing Bird hasn't stuck her bill in!
Tommy Pin Cushion, you might just as well keep out
of this—everybody knows you're stuck on yourself—
Fatty!"

Fatt.

"You conceited old Silver Thimble," came the
voice of Pin Cushion. "You will please address me
by my full name—'Tomato-Pin-Cushion, Custodian-
of-the-Sword-Needles';—and what's more, if you
don't quickly remove all those needles from poor
Emery, you won't get any more sword-needles to wield.
So there! You know Sewing Bird's taking forty
winks; that's why you don't act in your best military
manner."

Silver Thimble looked toward Sewing Bird, whose
eyes began to open, and quickly went toward Emery

"You conceited old Silver Thimble."

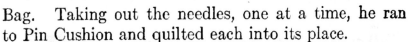

Bag.   Taking out the needles, one at a time, he ran
to Pin Cushion and quilted each into its place.

"There!" he exclaimed at length, "I'm certainly
glad I've 'stacked all my arms'—my, I'm tired!"
As he leaned back to yawn, off fell his helmet and he
melted away.

"Serves him right," murmured Emery Bag; "I
hope Fairy Lady won't ask him to the sewing
party to-day,—she really arranges all these lessons."

> "Don't fear! Don't fear!
>   Mr. Emery Bag;
> You've got Silv Thimble's
>   Very last tag,"

sang Sewing Bird.

"Good!" thought Mary Frances.   "Now, I'll go
in."

My. I'm glad I got that child to sleep

Chapter XII

Mary Frances' Treasure Box

"GOOD-AFTERNOON, dear Thimble People," said the little girl, putting Angie on a rocking chair.

"Good-afternoon," came many little voices, and Sewing Bird began to sing:—

"Oh, do you know,
Oh, do you know
What we have planned
For us to sew?"

"I don't," laughed Mary Frances. "Please tell me?"

"For your dear dolly we will make,
And every pains will try to take,
An apron, and a pinafore;
And later, other things galore;

An apron
and a
pinafore

[89]

Her wardrobe we so full will fill,
No one would care to pay her bill."

"Magic and Mystery!" exclaimed Mary Frances, putting her hands over her eyes; and Fairy Lady sat in the doll's rocking chair.

"Oh," said Mary Frances somewhat breathlessly, "excuse me for calling you so suddenly, but I so wanted to talk with another woman—" and then she blushed, fearing she had offended the little bird.

"And not a bird," smiled Fairy Lady. "I understand," she nodded, "a bird, be she ever so wise, doesn't understand the needs of a doll-child or the heart of her mother."

"Thank you, dear Fairy Lady," replied Mary Frances.

"And I know how brave you are while your mother is away, Mary Frances, child," continued Fairy Lady, "but I've had orders from our King not to speak of that—so we'll get the material ready for dolly's apron."

"Here is the lawn," said Mary Frances. "Grandma gave it to me."

"Thank you
dear
Fairy
Lady"

"Here is the lawn"

"By the way," said Fairy Lady. "Where will you put these things as you make them? You must keep them a secret, you know, until we finish the lessons, or we'll become Never-Nevers."

"I shall keep them in my treasure box. Mother gave it to me a year ago. It has a little key and it locks. Mother said all girls love to have a kind of a secret place to keep treasures in."

"Have you the box here?" asked Fairy Lady.

"Oh, yes," smiled Mary Frances. "I keep it in my trunk. It is made of tin, and very light."

"Go and get it, please."

"Good," laughed the sweet voice of Fairy Lady, as Mary Frances brought in the treasure box. "Now, everything is prepared."

"May I tell about the lovely lessons, sometime?" asked Mary Frances.

"Yes," smiled Fairy Lady. "You may,—some day. We do not want our help to be given to one little girl only—so when we are all through, you can form a Sewing Circle to which your girl friends may belong, and you can teach them all you have learned."

"Oh, how perfectly lovely!" exclaimed Mary

"Yes, some day"

Frances. "But won't you help me any more then,—you, and the dear, dear Thimble People?"

"You'll have your mother then, you know," explained Fairy Lady.

"Oh, yes," said Mary Frances happily. "She had planned to teach me to sew this very summer—it will be another grand surprise for her if I know how—when she comes."

"I wish afternoons were much longer," smiled Fairy Lady; "but we must do our lesson. Now, just a word

19.—ABOUT CLOTH, WEAVING, AND SPINNING

Cotton cloth is made from the cotton plant; wool cloth from sheep's fleece; silk cloth from silk worm's cocoon; linen cloth from the flax plant.

The soft cotton is the warm coat for the cotton plant seed-baby. The fleecy wool is the warm coat of the sheep, or the little lambs. The web from the silk worm's cocoon is the cradle in which it sleeps. Linen is made from the stalks of the flax plant.

When these materials are spun, or twisted, into long threads, we have spool cotton and silk, wool yarns, and linen thread, for sewing. When the threads are woven or laced together into cloth, the stronger threads run the length of the goods—they are the warp threads. The weaker, or woof threads, run crosswise of the goods.

"Good, now everything is prepared"

CHAPTER XIII

MAKING A DOLL'S APRON

"IN cutting any garment, wherever there will be a pull upon the goods, what threads should bear the strain?"

"The warp threads," answered Mary Frances, deeply interested.

"Good," said Sewing Bird Fairy Lady, "the warp threads, or lengthwise of the goods. Now, we are ready for

PATTERN 2.—DOLL'S APRON

1. Cut a piece of lawn five inches, lengthwise of the goods; and seven inches wide. You can pull out a thread and cut along the line it makes, to get a perfectly straight edge.

2. Cut two strings each six inches long, lengthwise of the goods, and one and one-half inches wide.

3. Cut a band four inches long, and two inches wide.

"How tall is your dolly?" she asked.

"I'll have to measure," said Mary Frances.

[93]

"The warp threads"

"Come," she said, "Angie, dear, wake up! Mother wants to see how big her dolly has grown."

Angie was very good and stood quite still while Mary Frances held her against the yardstick.

"Sixteen inches tall," she said; "nearly half a yard.'

"Then the apron will be just right," smiled Fairy Lady. "Now, I'll give you directions.

Making a Doll's Apron (Pattern 2)

1. Fold the two five-inch sides together, to find center. Clip a notch at the top.

2. Open. Turn an inch hem at the bottom, and baste it in place. Hem with No. 9 needle, and No. 60 or 70 white cotton.

3. Turn a quarter inch hem on the sides. Baste and hem.

"Next you gather the top, and set the gathers into the band; but first you must learn about

20.—Gathering

Gathering is done by the use of the running stitch.

1. Turn the goods over one-quarter of an inch from edge and pinch a crease to mark a line to follow with the gathering stitches. Open it up.

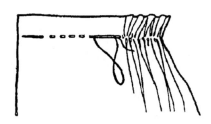

"Learn about gathering"

2. Use a thread a little longer than the space to be gathered, which is from the center notch to the side of the apron.

(Use No. 40 cotton for gathering the apron.)

3. Make a good-sized knot, put needle in downward on right side of goods.

4. Sew on crease, taking several stitches before pulling needle through. Aim to take up on the needle about half as many threads of the goods as you skip, but do not trouble to count them.

5. When finished, make a knot in the end of the thread and let it hang.

6. Put a pin in at the last stitch you took, and draw up the work a little, fastening the thread over and under the pin.

Stroke the gathers.

"Stroking is done to make the gathers set more evenly."

Fastenin
thre
over ar
uude
the pi

21.—STROKING OF GATHERS

1. With right side toward you, begin at left hand edge.

2. Hold work between the thumb and first finger of left hand. Keep thumb below gathering thread.

3. Put point of a blunt needle or eye of an ordinary needle under a little plait of the goods and bring it up under the thumb, draw needle down and pinch plait with thumb.

NOTE.—Stroking is not often done to very thin goods, lest it be torn, but many small stitches are placed on the needle at once and pinched together before pulling the thread through.

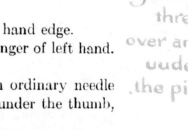

"Now the apron is ready for

22.—SETTING GATHERS IN A BAND

1. Find the middle of the band and clip a tiny notch in edge of each side.

2. Clip off each corner of band, to avoid thickness of goods.

3. Pin the right hand end of the gathered piece one-quarter of an inch from the right hand end of band.

4. Pin the center of the gathered piece to the center of the band.

5. Pin the left hand end of the gathered piece one-quarter of an inch from the left hand end of the band.

6. Tighten or loosen the gathering thread to the exact length of the band and fasten under and over the pin.

7. With needle point, distribute, or spread, the gathers evenly.

8. With gathers toward you, baste with small even basting stitch just above the gathering thread.

9. With stitching stitch, sew the gathering to the band, taking up one gather at a time. Fasten thread and cut off.

10. Turn up the band. Fold the opposite side over toward you one-quarter of an inch from the edge. Crease. Do the same to the ends of band.

11. Fold this over the gathers, bringing the folded edge just over the stitching.

Pinch together

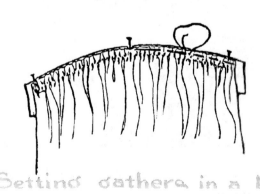

Setting gathers in a band

12. Pin the middle of the band to the middle of the stitching, and the ends to the ends, exactly even.

13. Baste, with even basting.

14. Hem the gathers against the band, taking up one gather at a time.   Do not let the stitches show on right side.

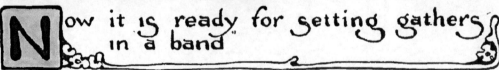

Now it is ready for setting gathers in a band

CHAPTER XIV

A LOAN FROM THE THIMBLE KING

"DEAR me," sighed Mary Frances. "How will I ever get so much done? I didn't want to interrupt you, dear Fairy Lady, but I've gotten, you see, no further than basting the hem of dolly's apron!"

Big tears trembled in the little girl's eyes.

"Dear child," smiled Fairy Lady. "We realize how rapidly we'll have to work in these lessons in order to get through before your mother comes, so we are ready to help."

With this, she rapped three times on the sewing table with her bodkin wand, whereat a little fellow of queer appearance walked solemnly up to Mary Frances and made a pompous bow.

"There is but one needle in the world, your Seamstress-ship," he said, "which is called the Needle-of-Don't-Have-to-Try, and the King of the Thimble

"Dear
me."

[98]

"There is but one needle in the world."

People has sent it to you by your humble servant,"
glancing proudly about.

"Why," said Mary Frances, scarcely daring to
breathe. "Why,—you, you are certainly my own
needle book!"

"Needle Book—that's my name,—and here, dear
Mistress, is the Needle-of-Don't-Have-to-Try."

Mary Frances saw a bright shiny light come from
between the opening leaves of Needle Book; then slowly,
very slowly, with his tiny little hand, he pulled out
what seemed a needle of fire, and dropping on his
knees, held it out on both arms toward Mary Frances.

The little girl hesitated. Would it burn her?

"Do not fear," smiled Fairy Lady. "It will not
harm you. The Needle-of-Don't-Have-to-Try is
loaned to you on only one condition: which is, that
you will promise to sew some time every day between
lesson days."

The little
girl
hesitated

"Oh, I promise," exclaimed Mary Frances. "I
do not, dear Sewing Bird Lady, I do not deserve such
beautiful kindness!"

She took the Needle-of-Don't-Have-to-Try from
Needle Book.

Held it out towards Mary Frances

"I do thank you—very—gratefully," she said, not knowing exactly how to behave toward the ambassador of the Thimble King.

"For shame, Tommy Pin Cushion!" exclaimed Fairy Lady, who overheard him mimicking Needle Book. "Don't make fun! Never, never will you be Bearer of the Needle-of-Don't-Have-to-Try for the King of Thimble Land."

"I beg your pudden!" said Tommy Pin Cushion to Needle Book, getting very red in the face.

"Poor Pinny!" exclaimed Needle Book, looking very disdainfully toward Tomato Pin Cushion, "always getting 'squelched!'"

"Poor Pinny"

"Come," said Fairy Lady. "No more of that needle-and-pin talk!" Then to Mary Frances:

"Now, little lady, you may begin. The next is

TO HEM DOLLY'S APRON STRINGS

1. Turn a very narrow hem the long way of the strings. Hem with fine hemming stitches.

2. Turn and make a half-inch hem at one end of each string.

"Shall I finish the apron first?" asked Mary Frances. "Shall—shall I use the new needle?"

"I beg your pudden"

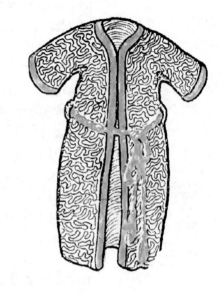

4. Night Gown 5. Bath-robe

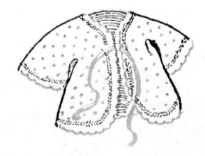

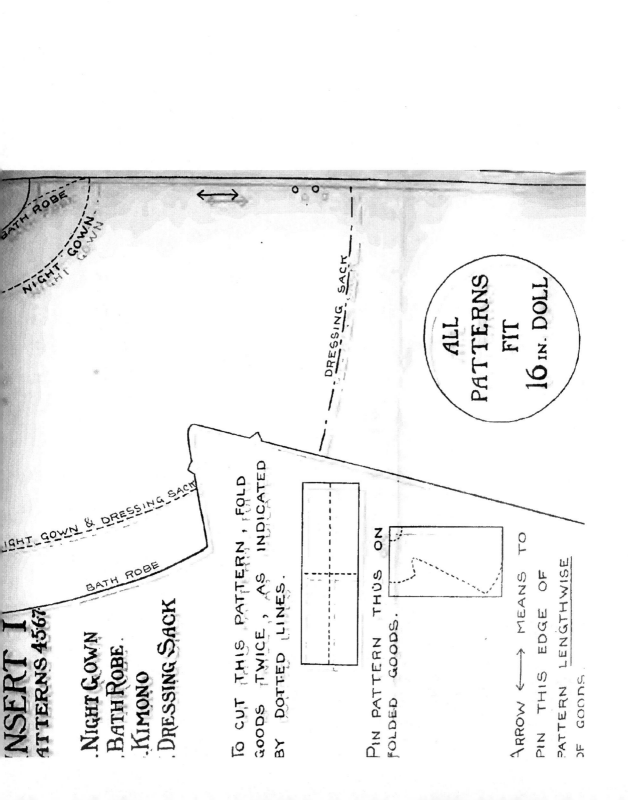

BATH ROBE

NIGHT GOWN

DRESSING SACK

ALL
PATTERNS
FIT
16 IN. DOLL

NIGHT GOWN & DRESSING SACK

BATH ROBE

INSERT I
PATTERNS 4·5·6·7·

NIGHT GOWN
BATH ROBE.
KIMONO
DRESSING SACK

TO CUT THIS PATTERN, FOLD GOODS TWICE, AS INDICATED BY DOTTED LINES.

PIN PATTERN THUS ON FOLDED GOODS.

ARROW ⟷ MEANS TO PIN THIS EDGE OF PATTERN LENGTHWISE OF GOODS.

INSERT I

PATTERNS 4·5·6·7·

- NIGHT GOWN
- BATH ROBE
- KIMONO
- DRESSING SACK

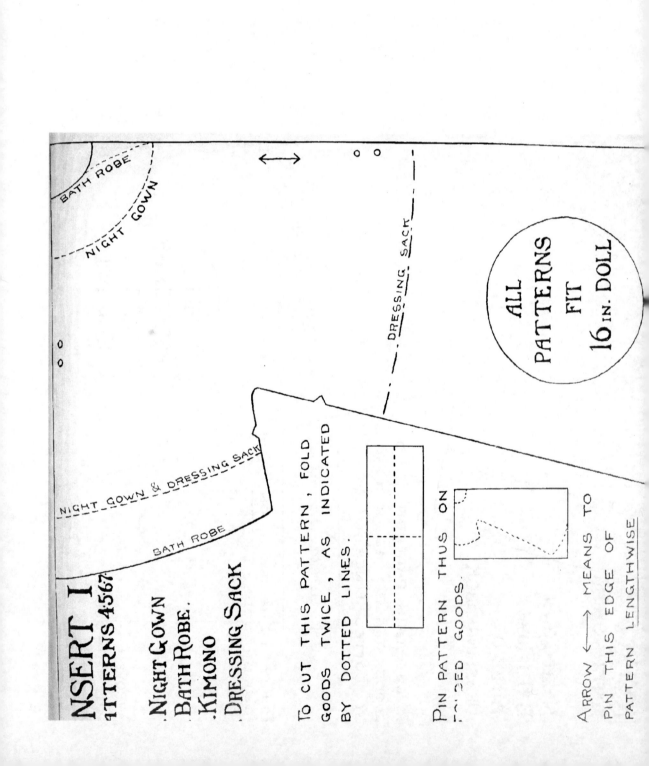

BATH ROBE

NIGHT GOWN

NIGHT GOWN & DRESSING SACK

BATH ROBE

DRESSING SACK

ALL PATTERNS FIT 16 IN. DOLL

TO CUT THIS PATTERN, FOLD GOODS TWICE, AS INDICATED BY DOTTED LINES.

PIN PATTERN THUS ON FOLDED GOODS.

ARROW ⟷ MEANS TO PIN THIS EDGE OF PATTERN <u>LENGTHWISE</u>

"Yes," smiled the delighted Fairy Lady.

Mary Frances found her thimble, and threaded the glowing needle, although she feared it would scorch the thread,—but it seemed like any other needle except that she didn't have to try twice to put in the thread.

"I wonder how it is diffcrent?" she thought as she started to sew.

Then the most wonderful thing happened. She found the needle darting ahead of her hand, making the stitches just as fast as she could touch the eye with her silver thimble.

In a minute the apron was hemmed.

In another minute the apron was gathered.

In another minute the strings were hemmed.

Then the Needle-of-Don't-Have-to-Try stopped dead still and wouldn't move.

"Oh! ho!" cried Mary Frances. "What have I done? What have I done?"

"Nothing, dear child," said Fairy Lady. "But the Needle-of-Don't-Have-to-Try cannot do for you anything you have not yet learned; so use your own needle and set the gathers of the apron into the band."

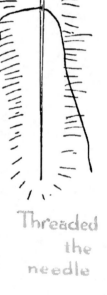

Threaded
the
needle

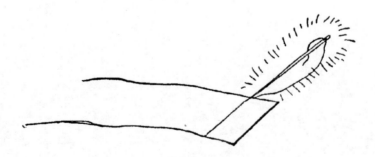

In a minute the strings were hemmed

"Thank you very much," said Mary Frances, finishing the apron band.

"And now," said Fairy Lady, "as to

PUTTING THE STRINGS INTO THE BAND

1. Gather, or lay small plaits at the unhemmed end of strings, and insert, or push them into the ends of the band.
2. Hem down."

"Well done, dear child," smiled Fairy Lady at length.

Then quicker than Mary Frances could wink, she turned into Sewing Bird, and began to sing,

"Oh, my! Oh, my! Oh, my! Oh, my!
It brings a twinkle to my eye!
The Needle-of-Don't-Have-to-Try!
Dear little miss, good-bye,
        Good-bye."

Dear little miss, good bye.
    Good bye"

CHAPTER XV

THREE LITTLE KITTENS

"THREE little kittens sitting in a row,
  All on a dolly's lap,
   Tit, tat, toe!"

sang Sewing Bird when Mary Frances came for the next lesson.

"Three in a row on a dolly's lap?" said Mary Frances. "Not my dolly's, I guess—she couldn't hold three."

Then sang Sewing Bird:

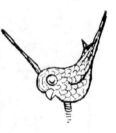

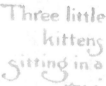

Three little
kittens
sitting in a
row

  "Come riddle me this,
   Come riddle me that,—
  Your dolly can hold
   A cat, and a cat, and a cat!"

"Why, how? oh, Magic and Mystery!" cried Mary Frances eagerly.

Then came Fairy Lady.

"This way," she smiled; "come, Pen Cil," and with a bound Pen Cil began to draw on the dolly's apron the picture of kittens given on this page.

(Any little girl can transfer this pattern to her **own** dolly's apron by using a carbon sheet.)

"Oh, how cute!" exclaimed Mary Frances.   "Yes, I think my dolly could hold three of those cats."

Fairy Lady smilingly continued, "Now, with the red working cotton and a canvas piece you may learn

23.—KENSINGTON OUTLINE STITCH

(Canvas 7 in. by 1½ in.)

utline
stitch

1. Begin at the left hand end of a piece of canvas.   Put needle in from under side.   Pull thread through.

2. Two threads over, put needle in downward and up through the hole next to the left, holding work over forefinger of left hand. Pull through.

3. Work from you, and always drop the thread on the same side of the needle.

"Now, try it on muslin.   You'll need an embroidery needle, because the large eye makes way for the heavy cotton."

Three Little Kittens

"Oh, I have one here in my basket, and some quite-a-bit finer working cotton, in pink,—isn't it pretty?"

"I—I—put it there," began Needle Book.

"Hush!" said Fairy Lady, holding up a finger. "Now, little Miss, see if you can make that stitch on muslin."

"Very good, indeed."

"Mary Frances! Mary Frances! Mary Frances!" came Grandma's voice from the hall.

With one leap, Fairy Lady changed to Sewing Bird, and all the other Thimble People, who had been standing on the sewing table, tumbled head-over-tin-cups into the sewing basket.

Tumbled into the basket

"Yes, Grandma," called Mary Frances, running out.

"Why, my dear," puffed the old lady, climbing the last of the stairs, "I am home very early, you see. There was no regular meeting to-day because almost all the members of the Ladies' Guild went to Daisy's wedding. I'm home for some games with my little girl."

"Oh, Nanny-dear, will you play 'Piddy-Pinny-Plump?'" asked Mary Frances.

"Mary Frances!"

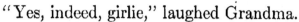

"Yes, indeed, girlie," laughed Grandma.

"Goody!" exclaimed Mary Frances.   "I'll be ready soon as ever I tidy up the sewing room."

"I'm sorry, dear Thimble People," she began. Then she heard the sweet bird voice of Sewing Bird. singing very softly,

"With outline stitch,
    So pretty and neat,
Outline the kitties,
    From head to feet;

"And have them done
    When next we meet,
And they will look,
    Sweet, sweet!   Sweet, sweet!"

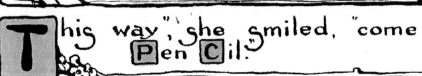

This way", she smiled, "come Pen Cil."

CHAPTER XVI

A SURPRISE FROM MOTHER

A SHARP ring at the door bell.

"A telegram for Miss Mary Frances," said Katie coming into the dining-room.

"A telegram! And for you, Mary Frances. What can it be!" exclaimed Grandma.

"Shall I sign for it, ma'am?" asked Katie.

"No," said Grandma. "Mary Frances better learn to sign for herself."

There was a little look of excitement in Grandma's face, and a little pink spot in each cheek.

Trembling with wonder, Mary Frances gravely wrote her name in the book. She opened the queer looking envelope, with printing almost all over its face, and read:

Telegram

Miss Mary Frances:

| *Expect* | *by* | *Express* | *Mary* | *Marie* | |
| *and* | *trunk.* | *Letter* | *follows.* | | |

Mother.

"Oh! Oh! Oh!" she cried. "I know, Nanny dear, I know! Mary Marie is my dear new dolly. I do wonder what she will be like! Isn't Mother too sweet and kind!"

"There's the postman," said Grandma, all laughter and smiles. "I wonder if he—" but Mary Frances was already at the door.

"Surely enough," she cried. "A letter from Father. I'll read it to you, Grandma—" tearing open the envelope:

A letter from Father!

Dear Mary Frances:—

Mother bought for you to-day the prettiest doll in San Francisco, and she is going to send it by express, as soon as she gets some shopping done for the young lady. She will send a telegram when she starts Mary Marie on her journey, and will write a letter of instruction as to her health, wealth, and happiness.

Give our love to dear Grandma.

It is a delight to send the prettiest doll in San Francisco, to the darlingest little girl in the whole wide world —at least she is to her

Loving Father.

"Your Father meant that to reach here before the telegram," said Grandma.

"San Francisco is so far off," said Mary Frances; "but, oh, Grandma, isn't it too lovely! Will Mary Marie have light hair and blue eyes, or dark hair and brown eyes, I wonder?"

"I wonder, too," smiled Grandma.

"I know she'll be pretty, for Mother has such superb taste, as Father says."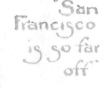

"Yes, dear," smiled Grandma.

"Oh, I can hardly wait," said the little girl, looking out of the window.

"Come, dear, finish your breakfast."

"May I tell Katie?"

"Yes," nodded Grandma.

Katie was as delighted as Mary Frances.

"Katie is a wonder, Nanny," said Mary Frances. "She was telling me yesterday about all she could do when she was little. When she was a mere child she could cook a pair of pork chops beautifully, she told me."

"But Katie is only eighteen, now," laughed, Grandma.

Katie was delighted

"That seems awfully old to me," said Mary Frances.

"Katie loves animals, too, Grandma," she went on, "and so do I! Last summer, Nanny, when Father had Josie Worrell and his horse plow our garden, I went out and patted the horse's nose.   He was so pleased, you should have seen him wag his tail."

Grandma laughed again.   "You have a dear, sweet heart, little girlie," she said; and taking Mary Frances by the hand, went out on the veranda.

You have a dear, sweet, heart

.   .   .   .

"Oh, Miss Mary Frances, here comes the expressman carrying a box!" exclaimed Katie a few mornings later.

"Katie, Katie, I'll go to the door," cried Mary Frances running down stairs.

"The dear, blessed dolly!" she exclaimed, taking the big package from the expressman.   "Nanny, I can hear her calling, almost."

"We'll have you out of the dark box soon, Mary Marie, dear," she whispered through an opening in the wrapping paper.

"Come, Katie, you help; we'll carry it where the wrapping will make no trouble, out in the kitchen—and

"Here comes the express——"

I'll bring the dolly for you to see, Nanny, dear, soon as she's unpacked."

"You cut the string, Miss," said Katie, "and I'll pry off the cover."

"Oh," exclaimed Mary Frances. "I never, never saw so much tissue paper—thirty, thirty-one, thirty-two, thirty-three, thirty-four sheets—when will I get to her! Oh, there she is! Isn't she a darling, Katie! And look, here's her trunk!"

Surely Mary Marie was a lovely doll. She had beautiful long curls tied with pink ribbon; and on her feet were short stockings and slippers,—but her dress was a very plain, simple, "slip" of lawn.

There was a note pinned on Mary Marie's dress, and a little key. The note read:

Dear Scout:

Please read my letter in the tray of Mary Marie's trunk before unpacking. Here is the key.

Surely
Mary Marie
was a lovel
doll

Mother.

"Oh, bring the trunk, please, Katie," said Mary Frances, "and I'll carry Mary Marie."

"Come, dear," she said.   "Mother wants to take you up to see Grandma and Angie, your sister."

Mary Marie nestled back in Mary Frances' arms, and closed her eyes quite contentedly.

"What lovely long eye-lashes," whispered Mary Frances.

After showing the dolly to Grandma, she unlocked the trunk and took out her mother's letter.

'Oh, listen! Grandma, listen!" she burst out. "I'll read it to you!"

Dear Mary Frances:

This is Mary Marie.   Isn't she lovely?   She is the very doll I've been looking for, for my own dear daughter. Father has told you something about Mary Marie, but I want to add some particulars.

I have nothing to say about the care of her,—for I know my little girl's careful, neat ways so well.   You may be surprised when you unpack her trunk, to find no dresses.   Mother is sending you, instead, all kinds of pretty goods which you may make up into dresses and clothes for your new little daughter; and you will find all kinds of laces and ribbons, and buttons, and hooks and

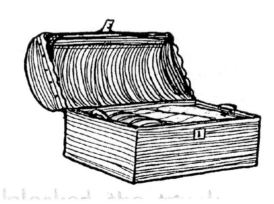

eyes—everything Mother could think Mary Frances or Mary Marie could possibly want.

There is a set of toilet articles,—but I'll not tell you about the other things, for I know you are anxious to find out for yourself.

I wish I could be with you, dear, to teach you how to make the pretty things; but I will, I hope, be able to do that before so very long. Meantime, I want you to use everything just as you wish. I've asked Grandma to let you do exactly as you want to with these things, and I ask you not to go to her with your sewing problems: for the doctor said that Grandma must not strain her eyes with any such work. I know you understand.

I hope, dear, Mary Marie will bring a little bit of such pleasure to her Mother as her Mother has brought to me.

With love, and a bear hug,   Mother.

P.S.—Expect to be home before long.

A set of toilet articles

"Oh, isn't it grand! Come on, Nanny, we'll unpack the trunk now!"

Soon the tray was out, and all the delightful contents were spread in view.

Soon the tray was out

"Isn't it wonderful!" said Grandma, almost as much pleased and excited as the little girl herself.

These are some of the things they found in Mary Marie's trunk:

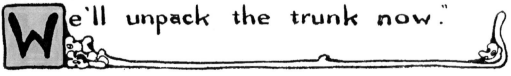

We'll unpack the trunk now."

CHAPTER XVII

MARY MARIE'S HANDKERCHIEF

MARY FRANCES watched for the first chance to show the Thimble People her mother's presents.

When she knew her grandma was napping, she ran breathlessly up to the sewing room, leaving Mary Marie and her trunk outside the door.

"Oh, Thimble People," she said, "listen! I can scarcely wait to tell you about the delightful surprise Mother has sent me. It is too beautiful—and you can all share it with me! Guess what it is! Guess!"

"That's easy!" said Scissors Shears excitedly, "it's a plow!"

"A plow!" exclaimed Emery Bag. "What a silly thing! What put that in your head?"

"What else has a share, I'd like to know? Little Miss said she'd 'share it'—and I've heard of a plow-share—and so there! Rip-him-up! I say, Rip-him-up-the-back!"

"It's a plow!"

[115]

Scissors Shears gave a kick toward Emery Bag.

"For shame!" said Mary Frances. "Now be good, Scissors Shears; and all guess again."

"I give it up!" sighed Scissors Shears.

"I'll tell you!" said Mary Frances. "No, I guess I'll show you! Now, Thimble People, look! look!" she exclaimed, bringing in Mary Marie and holding her up before Sewing Bird.

"Oh, lovely beauty!
Lovely thing!
And can it sing,
Oh, can it sing?"

"No," laughed Mary Frances, "I don't believe she can!"

"Oh, what's her name?
Oh, what's her name?
Oh, will she run
Or is she tame?"

asked Sewing Bird.

"Very impolite," whispered Scissors Shears to

Holding her up before Sewing Bird

8. Pinafore

9. Morning Dress

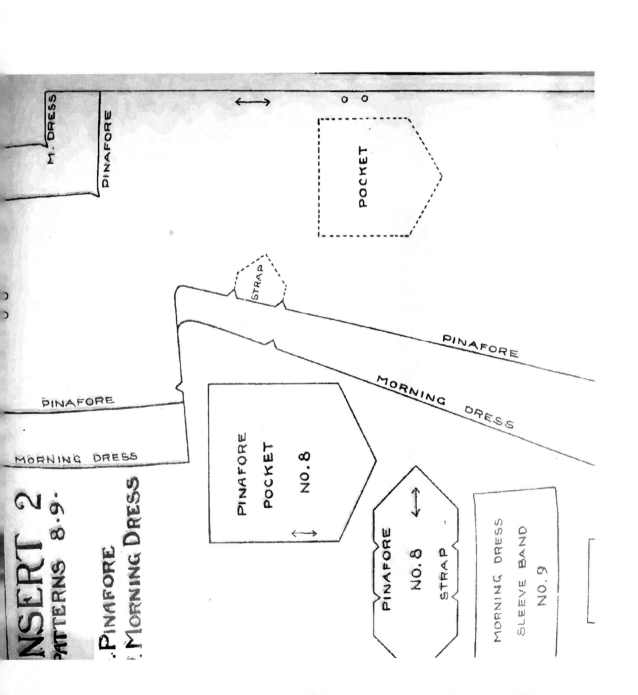

INSERT 2
PATTERNS 8·9·
PINAFORE
MORNING DRESS

M. DRESS

PINAFORE

POCKET

STRAP

PINAFORE

MORNING DRESS

PINAFORE

MORNING DRESS

PINAFORE
POCKET
NO. 8

PINAFORE
NO. 8
STRAP

MORNING DRESS
SLEEVE BAND
NO. 9

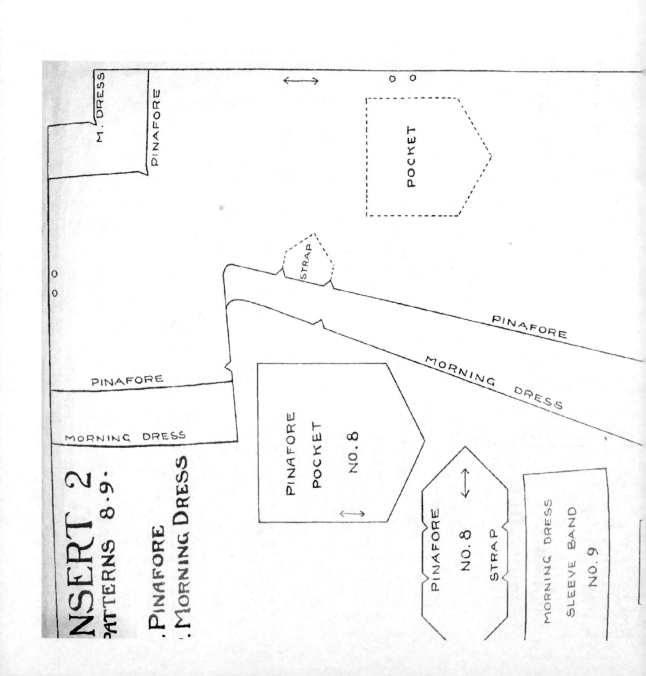

INSERT 2
PATTERNS 8·9·

PINAFORE
MORNING DRESS

POCKET

STRAP

PINAFORE

MORNING DRESS

PINAFORE

MORNING DRESS

PINAFORE
POCKET
NO. 8

PINAFORE
NO. 8
STRAP

MORNING DRESS
SLEEVE BAND
NO. 9

M. DRESS

PINAFORE

Tommy Pin Cushion, "to call anybody, 'What's-her-name.' "

"This," said Mary Frances, pretending she did not hear, "this, Thimble People, is Mary Marie."

> "A sweet little dolly
>   Is Mary Marie!
> As pretty a dolly
>   As ever could be.
>
> "She's not only sweet,
>   But tidy and neat
> From the top of her head
>   To the soles of her feet;
>
> "But she's full of real woes—
>   From her head to her toes
> She sadly needs stitching
>   And making of clothes,"

"Very impolite" whispered Scissors Shears

sang Sewing Bird.

"She certainly does, dear Magic and Mystery," laughed Mary Frances. Then to Fairy Lady,—"and I shall need your help so much! I'm simply too excited

to tell you rightly about all the rest of my perfectly beautiful surprise—but I will try."

Then she told of Mary Marie and her trunk.

"Bring in the trunk,—will you, please?" asked Fairy Lady, who had come at once, in answer to the magic word.

"Yes, indeed!" said Mary Frances; "I'm the richest mother, I guess, in the world, with such beautiful goods, dear Thimble People—oh, such a wonderful lot!"

Then she brought in the trunk and spread out all its pretty contents before the admiring eyes of the Thimble People.

"'m the
ichest
lother in
he world"

"It makes me sing
　As on the wing,
　　Though now I'm not a birdie;
　I'll break in song
　And sing so long
　　No one can say a wordie—

if I don't look out," sang Fairy Lady, "with such lovely goods to use for our lesson!   But to-day's lesson, little Miss, is to make a dolly's handkerchief.   You must first learn

"It makes me sing"

24.—HEM-STITCHING ON CANVAS

(Size: seven and one-half inches by two and one-half inches)

1. Draw out one group of threads one inch from edge of canvas.

2. Turn a hem to meet open space and baste with white cotton.

3. Thread needle with red cotton and begin at right hand side as for hemming, keeping the hem at the top.

4. Point needle toward you; put needle under one group of cross threads and pull through.

5. Put needle back and under same group of threads, and point it through the fold of the hem. Pull through.

To make

PATTERN 3.—DOLL'S HANDKERCHIEF

Cut a five-inch square of linen and prepare to do

HEM-STITCHING ON LINEN

1. One-half inch from the edge of the cloth, with the point of a needle, pick out and draw a coarse thread; then draw several more next to it.

2. Do the same to the other sides.

3. Now, turn a hem each side to meet the open space, and baste.

4. Hem-stitch with number sixty cotton.

Cut
Square
of linen

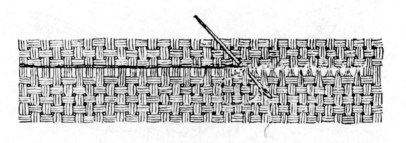

Hem-stitching

"If we were not here to help you, dear little Miss, you'd have to wait until you were much bigger before doing hem-stitching, for it is quite a strain on the eyes.

"You may do the canvas hem-stitching; then use the Needle-of-Don't-Have-to-Try for making dolly's handkerchief. Otherwise, you could simply hem the edges of the cloth, and learn about

25.—Sewing on Lace Edging

If lace is to be put on quite full, measure the distance on which it is to be sewed, and allow one and one-half times that distance in lace.

1. Place the right side of the lace to the right side of the cloth. Baste lightly, along one side. Overhand—beginning one-half inch from end of lace.

2. To turn a corner, measure the width of the lace, and allow twice the width, and pin a quarter of an inch beyond the corner. Overhand around the corner. Finish and allow one-half an inch on end of lace beyond sewing. Cut off.

Note.—Valenciennes Lace has a heavy thread woven in the top on which the fullness may be drawn. A gathering thread should be run in lace without such a thread.

4. To join the ends of lace you must learn about making a fell.

"What is a fell?" asked Tommy Pin Cushion.

"A fell's a fellow," solemnly declared Scissors Shears.

"For shame!" exclaimed Fairy Lady.

"What does 'fell' mean?" persisted Tommy Pin Cushion.

"It means he fell down," said Scissors Shears.

"Silly!" exclaimed Needle Book. "How could anybody 'fell down?'"

"Down is entirely too soft to fell!" said Tommy Pin Cushion.

"This is all foolish nonsense!" smiled Fairy Lady. "Let's proceed to make the felled seam."

"Excuse me!" exclaimed Scissors Shears, "but how does a fell seem?"

"It seems you seem to seem not to be what you seem to be!" laughed Tommy Pin Cushion.

"What's that?" demanded Scissors Shears sharply.

"A—a seemly fellow!" said Tommy Pin Cushion, giggling.

Everybody laughed.

"You interrupted me," said Fairy Lady, "in telling about

26.—MAKING A FELL

Cut two pieces of muslin, five inches long and two inches wide.

1. Place the two pieces together, one one-eighth of an inch below the other. Baste with uneven basting.

2. Sew together with Combination Stitch. (Two running stitches and a back stitch.)

3. Take out the basting, and open the pieces of cloth, and lay the seam over so that the wider edge will be on the top.

4. Turn this in over the narrow edge, and hem.

Lace is joined in the same way.

I did
it with
my little
helmet

"Oh, I see, Fairy Lady. That is so that no raw edges will show," exclaimed Mary Frances.

"Good!" smiled Fairy Lady. "Now, to hem-stitch the handkerchief."

"Where did I put that square of lovely linen?" said Mary Frances. "Oh, I left it in the work basket. Why—why, look, dear Fairy Lady, look—it is all cut and hem-stitched."

"How did this happen?" asked Fairy Lady.

"I did it with my little helmet," answered a little voice.

Making a Fell

"Thimble!" exclaimed Mary Frances.

"Thimble, what did you answer first for?" cried a sharp voice. "I started it!"

"Oh, Scissors!" said Mary Frances.

"Oh, for shame,—to quarrel before our little Miss—" began Tommy Pin Cushion.

"Oh, you turned good, have you, Tommy Pin Cushion!" exclaimed Scissors Shears.

"I had the honor, your Seamstress-ship," said Tomato Pin Cushion, "to furnish the 'Needle-of-Have-to-Try' for this work."

"Ha! Ha!" laughed Needle Book. "That's a joke."

"We did have to try hard," said Thimble, "to get it done so soon."

"I thank you all, dear Thimble People," said Mary Frances.

"Will you sew on the lace edging and bring it next time?" asked Fairy Lady.

"I will,—" said Mary Frances, "Oh, I haven't shown you the outlined kitties. Aren't they good?"

"Splendid!" exclaimed Fairy Lady.

"Ha! Ha!"

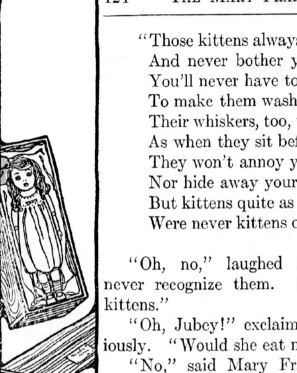

"Those kittens always will be good
And never bother you for food;
You'll never have to lay down laws
To make them wash their heads and paws;
Their whiskers, too, will stand out straight
As when they sit before the grate;
They won't annoy you with their noise
Nor hide away your pretty toys;
But kittens quite as good as that
Were never kittens of a cat."

"Oh, no," laughed Mary Frances. "Jubey'd never recognize them. She'd not know they were kittens."

"Oh, Jubey!" exclaimed Sewing Bird Lady, anxiously. "Would she eat me?"

"No," said Mary Frances. "Not Jubey. She never looks at Dick Canary."

"Oh, I forgot," said Fairy Lady, "I am a bird without feathers, and Jubey wouldn't care for a bird that didn't tickle her nose."

A sweet little dolly
Is Mary Marie!"

CHAPTER XVIII

A Nightie for her Little Nap

"A CHARMING thing
To make Marie,
Will be a dainty
White nightie,"

"White
nightie"

sang Sewing Bird.

"Oh, good!" exclaimed Mary Frances. "That is just what she needs. I had to loan her Angie's best one; and Angie's terribly cross. You see, I fear she is a little jealous of my new dolly. I'll not neglect Angie, but you understand, dear Sewing Bird Lady, that it is my duty to clothe this child—" anxiously—"Isn't that perfectly right?"

"What would she wear? What would she wear
Without a loving mother's care?
She'd freeze with every winter's breeze,
She'd die of shame if any tease;—
For every thinking body knows
No doll is glad without fine clothes."

[125]

"Thank you, Magic and Mystery," said Mary Frances.

"And," smiled Fairy Lady, "the Thimble People have been quite busy since last lesson—see?" She pulled from under the cushion of the doll's chair a paper pattern.

"Oh, how lovely!" exclaimed Mary Frances, clapping her hands. "A real pattern just such as Mother uses when she makes my dresses? What is this pattern to be used for?"

"For a dolly's nightgown," replied Fairy Lady, smiling happily. "Now, the materials required are:

Three-quarters of a yard of lawn, or muslin. Long-cloth is a very nice kind of muslin to use.
Three-quarters of a yard of lace ribbon beading.
One yard baby ribbon.

"Oh, how lovely!"

"Here they are!" said Mary Frances, hunting among the treasures in Mary Marie's trunk.

"They are perfectly all right," smiled Fairy Lady.

"Even to a fairy?" laughed Mary Frances.

"Even to a fairy," nodded Fairy Lady.

"Now, see if you can cut out

A paper pattern

PATTERN 4.—DOLL'S NIGHTGOWN

See Insert I

Follow the directions on the folded sheet.
To cut out—

1. Fold the lawn crosswise.

2. Lay edge of the pattern having the two rings (oo) on the folded edge of the lawn.

3. Cut out, being careful to clip the little V-shaped notches before removing the pattern.

NOTE.—*Always clip a small gash* in the corner under arm of these kimono-style dresses.

It took Mary Frances some time to fold the goods and pin the pattern on most carefully. So anxious was she to begin cutting out that she didn't notice Scissors Shears looking at her most beseechingly.

"If only—" he whispered—"if only—" but Sewing Bird Fairy Lady gave him an indignant push with her bodkin wand.

"The little lady must learn how," she said.

"Of course, of course," said Scissors Shears in a whisper, clicking off the words sharply, "but I want to help—"

"You'll help if you lend yourself—"

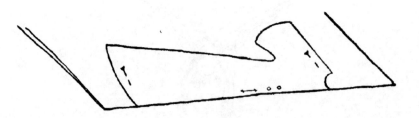

Lay edge of pattern on folded edge of lawn

"Lend myself," said Scissors Shears. "Now I might lend some one else. I could lend Bod Kin, for instance."

"Bod Kin!" exclaimed Mary Frances, catching the last words. "Is he a Thimble person?"

"He was!" sighed Scissors Shears, letting several tears fall.

"But," explained Fairy Lady, "one day he refused to do as the King commanded, and would not go through the muslin—so the King changed him into a blunt-nosed needle; and he has been compelled to be good ever since, even without his own consent."

"Poor Bod Kin!" said Scissors Shears, turning over so sharply that everybody jumped,

"Is he a Thimble person?"

"Poor Bod Kin,
    He didn't win;
        It is a sin,
            Thin as a pin,
                Can't make a din—
                    Poor old Bod Kin!
                        If I were he
                            And he were I,
                                He wouldn't be he
                                    And I wouldn't be I."

"Poor Bod Kin"

"Hee-hee," tinkled the silvery voice of Silver Thimble. "If you get too bright, you'll try to cut things out with one leg, Mr. Scissors."

"Come," said Fairy Lady, "Miss Mary Frances, your Seamstress-ship, will you please begin to cut the goods?"

"Lend yourself!" whispered Tomato Pin Cushion to Scissors Shears.

"Tommy Pin Cushion, you're stuck up!" clicked Scissors Shears, walking across the sewing table.

"I'll cut by the pattern most carefully, dear Sewing Bird Lady," said Mary Frances.

"Come," taking Scissors Shears up quite carelessly. "Just like a grown up lady," she thought as she cut out the little nightgown, and proudly held it up to the view of the Thimble People.

"Beautiful!" they cried.

"Not so beautiful as it will be," said Fairy Lady, "when it

"Lend yourself!"

> Has lace and ribbon,
> And ribbon and lace,
> Holding the lovely
> Things in place."

"Beautiful!"

"Oh," said Mary Frances. "I can scarcely wait!"

"Well, then," said Fairy Lady, "let us begin by learning a neat method of putting two materials together when the edges fray easily. It is called a

27.—FRENCH SEAM

1. Put the wrong sides of two pieces of goods against each other.
2. Baste about one-eighth of an inch from edge.
3. Sew with running stitch near the basting. Remove basting.
4. Turn the goods the other side out, and baste so as to enclose the seam.
5. Stitch with half-backstitching.

French
Seam

"Now, let us see what the nightgown looks like?"
Mary Frances held it up.

"Good!" said the Fairy Lady.   "Next you'll learn

TO MAKE DOLL'S NIGHTGOWN.—(PATTERN 4.)

1. Fold the two long halves together, and pin the notches against each other.
2. Baste carefully along this edge, and try on dolly. Alter, if necessary.
3. With running stitch, sew near the basting.
4. Turn to other side and baste seam carefully to enclose the first seam—a French Seam.
5. Sew with half-backstitching. Turn to right side.

"Good!" said Fairy Lady

"Do you recognize the French Seam?"

"Indeed I do," smiled Mary Frances.

"You may use the Needle-of-Don't-Have-to-Try for this lesson," said Fairy Lady, "because you've already learned these stitches.   Doesn't it pay to work patiently at first?"

"Oh, I'm the gratefulest child," said Mary Frances, taking from Needle Book the shining needle, which seemed almost too precious to use, and beginning to sew.

In a twinkle the French seams were neatly made.

"Now," said Fairy Lady, "fold a three-quarter of an inch hem at the bottom, and baste.   Then hem it."

The hemming the Needle-of-Don't-Have-to-Try quickly did.

"Ready," continued Fairy Lady, "for

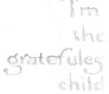

I'm the gratefulest child

Finishing the Neck

Clip a half dozen little slashes in the edge of the neck, and turn back to the right side of the goods one-quarter of an inch. Baste.

Turn back one-quarter of an inch the end of the lace beading ior ribbon, and baste it over the turned back goods, beginning in the center of the back.

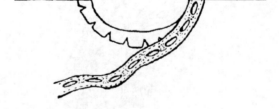

To finish neck

Cut off the lace beading one-quarter of an inch beyond the place it meets the beginning, and finish by turning it in one-quarter of an inch.   Hem beading down on lower edge.

FINISH THE SLEEVES

in the same way, but it is not necessary to slash them.   Then sew by overhanding stitch, some Valenciennes lace in neck and sleeves.   Join ends of the lace by a fell.

Thread
Bod Kin
with
ribbon

"Is that right?" asked Mary Frances at length.

"Good," smiled Fairy Lady.   "Now thread Bod Kin with the pretty baby ribbon, and run it in and out of the lace beading."

"Not your fairy wand!" exclaimed Mary Frances, hesitating to take hold of the bodkin wand Fairy Lady was holding out to her.

"For those who try," smiled Fairy Lady, "no gift of the fairies is too good.   Be sure to commence to run the ribbon in at the center of the front," she added, as Mary Frances took up Bod Kin.   "And leave ends long enough to tie pretty big bows."

"Isn't it a darling!" exclaimed the little girl, holding up the white nightgown.   "Now to try it on Mary Marie."

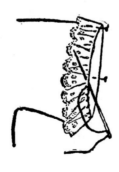

11. Underwaist

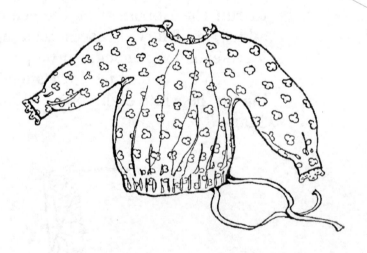

19. Guimpe

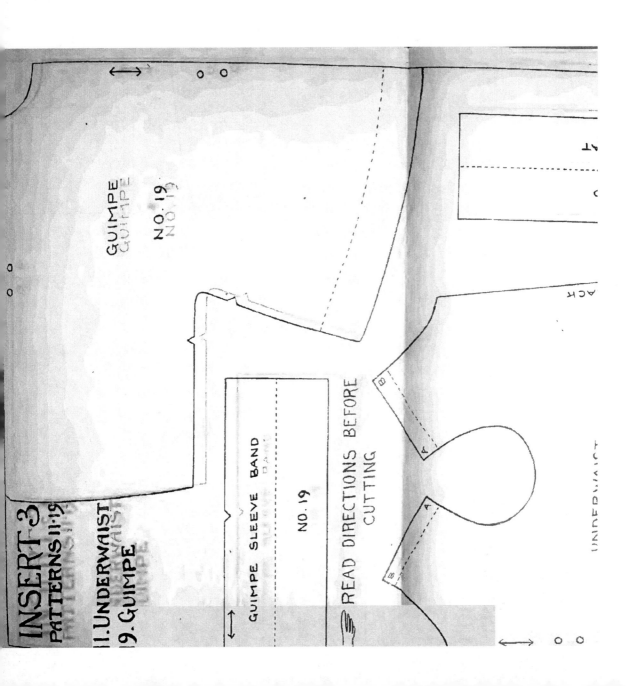

INSERT 3
PATTERNS 11-19

11. UNDERWAIST
19. GUIMPE

GUIMPE

NO. 19

GUIMPE SLEEVE BAND

NO. 19

READ DIRECTIONS BEFORE CUTTING

UNDERWAIST

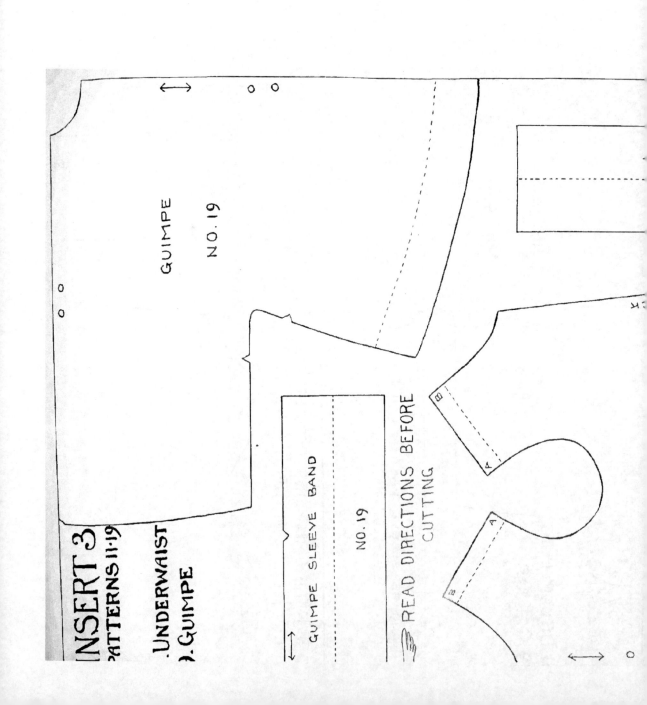

INSERT 3

PATTERNS 11-19

UNDERWAIST

GUIMPE

GUIMPE

NO. 19

GUIMPE SLEEVE BAND

NO. 19

READ DIRECTIONS BEFORE CUTTING

"Draw the ribbon to fit her neck and arms," said Sewing Bird Fairy Lady, "and tie the bows."

"Sweet Mary Marie!" sighed Mary Frances, looking at the lovely doll. "You ought to sleep well in such a pretty nightie! Isn't it beautiful!"

.   .   .   .

"Oh, dear me!"

Such a sigh!

Mary Frances looked up in surprise. Fairy Lady was gazing at Mary Marie with a sad, wistful look.

"Why, dear Fairy Lady," exclaimed Mary Frances, "what's the matter?"

"Nothing, my dear, so very queer," said the Fairy Lady smiling; "only that nightgown is just my size."

"Oh," exclaimed Mary Frances. "So it is! You can have it, dear Fairy Lady. I'll work and work to make Mary Marie another. Do take it!"

"No, thank you, dear little Miss," said Sewing Bird Lady,

"Oh, dear me!"

> "I've lovely fairy robes galore,
>   A thousand, and perhaps some more,—

Sweet Mary Marie

But when I see your loving care,
I'd be your dolly—I declare
I really think I would;—but, there!
I hear your grandma on the stair—
    Peep!"

You ought to sleep well in such a pretty nightie!"

CHAPTER XIX

HER BATH ROBE

"IF only in her nightie clad,
  She took a cold, 'twould be too bad—
  And so the dear child may not freeze,
  And so the dear child may not sneeze,
  A nice warm bath robe next will be
  Our lesson finished—"

Sewing Bird stopped singing.

"Brought to she," interrupted the tinkling voice of Silver Thimble.

"Silv Thimble!" exclaimed Sewing Bird, "when I need help, I'll call upon you—"

"Magic and Mystery!" laughed Mary Frances.

"Oh, dear Fairy Lady," said she. "Is it true— is it true—a bath robe for Mary Marie?"

"Yes," smiled Fairy Lady. "Here is

[135]

PATTERN 5.—DOLL'S BATH ROBE

See Insert I

To cut out—

1. Cut in the same way as nightgown, using the pattern marked BATH ROBE.

2. Remove pattern from material.

3. On the pattern, find the pinholes pricked along the neck line.

Cut down *one* row of these pinholes.

Fold the paper back along the other row of pinholes.

4. Spread open the bath robe.

Pin pattern in place on *one thickness* of material.

Cut along the V-shaped neck line.

Remove pattern.

5. Continue to cut the V-shaped neck to the bottom of the robe.

This makes the front opening.

"Pin it to the goods. Cut it out most carefully."

"But what goods shall I use, dear teacher?" asked Mary Frances, searching in Mary Marie's trunk.

"Oh, look, here is some lovely light blue eider-down flannel."

"Just the thing!" exclaimed Fairy Lady.

Continue V shaped opening to bottom

"Is there any ribbon to match?" peering over the table edge to look into the trunk.

"Too narrow," as Mary Frances held some up.

"There!" pointing down into the tray of the trunk, "that Dresden figured, pink and blue, inch wide ribbon is beautiful, and there must be about a yard and three-quarters of it."

"Lovely!" exclaimed Mary Frances, putting it with the flannel on the table. "Now, I'll cut out the bath robe."

"Very important! Very important!" whispered Tommy Pin Cushion as Scissors Shears came dancing, first on one leg and then on the other, to the edge of the table.

"I can't bother with you," whispered Scissors Shears, looking cross-eyed at Tommy Pin Cushion, "I've too much to go through," glancing up to see if Mary Frances noticed; but the little girl was smoothing out and pinning the pattern in place, and did not seem to hear.

"Oumph!" groaned Scissors Shears, as Mary Frances cut into the thick fabric.

"Bite into it hard, Scissors!" laughed Tommy Pin

"I can't bother with you"

"Very important!"

Cushion, but Fairy Lady silenced him with a wave of her wand.

"All cut out, and so well!" she said.

Scissors Shears looked pleased, as Mary Frances laid him down on the table.

Then Fairy Lady told how

To Make Doll's Bath Robe.—(Pattern 5.)

1. Pin seams together, being certain to match notches.
2. Baste. Try on doll. Alter, if necessary.
3. Stitch, or use combination stitch (two running stitches and a back-stitch).
4. Overcast, or blanket-stitch the raw edges of the seams.
5. Fold inch wide ribbon, and slip it over the raw edges of the bath robe—that is, the fronts and neck, and the sleeves.
6. To fit ribbon around curves, gather it a short distance on the fuller edge.

Pin seams together

When ready to cut ribbon, allow one-half inch for folding under when finishing.

Hem ends down carefully.

7. With sewing silk to match the ribbon, sew it to the robe, with small "in and out" stitches, slanting the needle slightly each time. Pull needle through to wrong side, then through to right side with each stitch—just as you did first stitches in canvas work.
8. Turn bottom of robe up one inch. Baste.

Catch-stitch with close stitches.

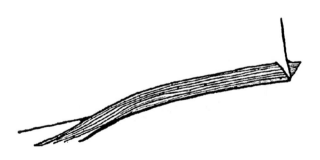

Slip ribbon over raw edges.

Mary Frances worked quietly for some time. "But how will my child fasten her bath robe?" she asked at length.

"Oh," said Fairy Lady. "That's a good question! Now learn,

28.—To Sew on Hooks and Eyes

No. 36 cotton, No. 7 needle. Two pieces muslin three inches by three inches. Fold in half. Baste edges.

The Eye

1. Place the eye a little beyond the double edge of the muslin. Hold firmly.

2. Overhand around the circles of the eye, beginning at the further side. Try not to let stitches come out on other side of the cloth.

3. Take three stitches at each side of the eye near edge of the cloth to prevent its being lifted when the hook is pulled. Fasten thread carefully in cloth near the eye.

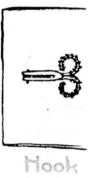

Hook

The Hook

1. Put the hook into the eye, facing it upward.

2. Take the other piece of muslin and place double edge just meeting the double edge of the first piece. Hold the hook down on this piece of muslin where it should come. Mark the place and now unfasten the hook from the eye.

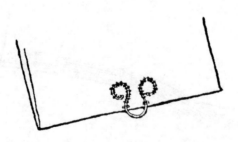

3. Hold hook firmly in place with left thumb and fingers, and overhand the two circles of the hooks.

4. Put needle under the bent part of hook and take four stitches in the same place, just under the bent part.

5. Fasten the thread by taking three stitches close beside the hook, then take three stitches on the other side close to hook. This secure fastening must be made because of the strain which comes on this part of the hook.

NOTE: If the eye will show on a garment it is better

eye showing

29.—TO MAKE EYELET LOOPS

Use a piece of muslin three inches square. Fold in half, and baste edges. No. 7 needle; No. 36 cotton.

1. Knot the thread.

2. One-half an inch from double edge, take four stitches about one-quarter of an inch long, over each other; bring needle out at lower end.

3. Turn the cloth and make blanket stitches over the four stitches. It is more easily done if the eye, instead of the point of the needle, is put through the long stitches.

4. When the stitches are filled with the blanket stitch, bring needle to wrong side of goods near the last blanket stitch taken and fasten securely.

"As we have so little time at a lesson, your Seam-stress-ship," said Fairy Lady, "you will please prac-

Eyelet loop

tice making the loops and putting on the hooks and
eyes during the week.

"A pretty cord for her waist is made by placing two
strands of heavy zephyr yarn together, and twisting
each end the opposite way.   There, I see some charming
blue in the trunk!   You may cut two pieces, each two
yards long, and place them together.   I will hold them
at one end.   You, at the other.   Now, ready:

> The ends in *your* hand, *left* you twist;
> To the *right*, I turn *mine* with the wrist;
> By the *center*, *I* hold the twisted strand:
> Let go!   A rope for dolly,—grand!
> A knot in each end next we tie,
> Then fringe each end, both you and I.
> A girdle for a queen not neater,
> No queen than dolly could be sweeter."

"Isn't that a lovely girdle!" exclaimed Mary
Frances.

"It is!" agreed Fairy Lady, "and now, with the
Needle-of-Don't-Have-to-Try, finish the bath robe,
ready for tacking the girdle in place."

Twisting each end opposite way

"It's the loveliest thing I've ever made," cried Mary Frances, holding up the soft woolly robe to view, "and it's all finished for my darling Mary Marie,—except the hook and eye."

"Not quite," said Sewing Bird Fairy Lady; "we like to teach little girls to be neat,—and how can Mary Marie hang up her clothes without

Its the loveliest thing!

30.—LOOPS OF TAPE

Flat Loops

Flat loops are sewed to inside of coat or waist collar, or skirt bands.

1. Cut narrow tape one-half an inch longer than the right length for the space in which it is to be used.

2. Turn under the ends one-quarter of an inch, and baste in place.

3. Hem down each end on three sides, the width of the tape.

4. Sew with a double row of stitching across the tape just beyond the hemming.

Towel Loops

Are used on towels and on inside of sleeves.

1. Fold tape to form a point.

Flat loops

2. Overhand the two ends together in center, for a distance of three-quarters of an inch from the ends.

3. Turn back the two ends one-quarter of an inch, and baste to the hemmed edge of towel, or muslin, and hem down.

4. Turn to right side. Hem down the cloth to the tape at the lower edge of the hem. Fasten thread.

'Of course," exclaimed Mary Frances. "Why, my dear Sewing Bird Lady, I couldn't be neat myself without 'hangers.'"

"Neither can Mary Marie," sang Sewing Bird.

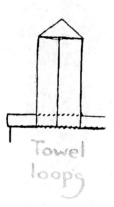

Towel loops

"Could she be sweet,
   Could she be neat,
From her dear head
   To her cute feet;
Without the stitches
   Made with care,
Without a comb
   For her fair hair,
Without some mending
   Of her clothes,
Without clean hankies
   For her nose,

Without a patient
   Mother's sewing?
But hark! Dear friend,
   You must be going!
     Peep-Peep!"

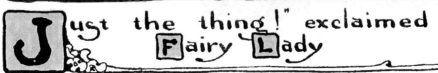

Just the thing!" exclaimed Fairy Lady

CHAPTER XX

Ma Chine

THE sun shone brightly into the sewing-room; everything was neatly in place. Sewing Bird was sitting on her perch on the sewing table. Mary Frances' work basket was at one end.

That is the way things looked as Mary Frances peeped in the door to see what the Thimble People might be doing.

She was just about to enter, when she saw a little fluttering in the work basket.

"Oh, I do hope they'll have some fun," she thought.

Over the edge of the basket peeped the bright little eyes of Silver Thimble. Then he tumbled out on the sewing table.

"Why didn't you step over, Silv?" asked Scissors Shears, stepping over the side of the basket.

"I'll take steps to find out why," said Tommy Pin Cushion, rolling over the side.

"You'll take steps! Impossible!" exclaimed Emery

Sewing
Bird
on her
perch

[145]

Bag.   "Why, Fatty, I could get out of the basket as easily as that myself!"   And out he jumped.

Then out came Pen Cil, carrying a little piece of paper.

"What's that for?" asked Silver Thimble, pointing to the paper.

"What do you 'spose, Tinkle?" he asked, loftily looking down upon the little fellow—"to write on."

"Oh, I ought to have known," snickered Silver Thimble.   "You always do write!"

"I am the only one of you who does, though," and Pen Cil hopped on his one leg to the other end of the table.   Jumping up and down, he began:

"All ready for the grand presentation?   Let's practice!"

"Not so fast!   Not so fast!   Mr. Pen Cil," exclaimed Needle Book.   "I lead!"

"Oh, beg your pardon," said Pen Cil.   "I forgot! I'm lead—ah, I've always been lead," sighing.

"Ha!   Ha!" laughed Tommy Pin Cushion, "tied to his miss's apron-strings!"

'But where are the rest of us?" called out Scissors Shears.

With that, out sprang all the needles and pins—
even a few safety pins Mary Frances had put in one
corner of her work box; all the buttons, and all the
other little findings; so many, Mary Frances couldn't
see where they came from.

Then Sewing Bird, who had been looking on with
interest, began to sing:

> "Now, listen here,
>   This must be clear:
>   This Presentation Party
>   Is for our little Mistress dear—
>   Look out, there, Mr. Smarty!"

as Scissors Shears nearly tumbled off the table.

> "I will take
>   The lady's place,
>   And you will pass
>   Before my face
>   As when she's here,
>   Our Mistress dear,
>   At our Presentation Party

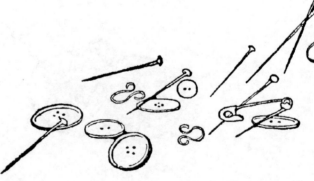

Out sprang all the small findings.

"Now, I will make
My little speech,
Then you can follow
One and each—"

"Except," interrupted Silver Thimble, "the tiny Tom Thumb Thimble Folks," drawing himself up to his full height.

"They only bow—
They all know how,"

said Sewing Bird.
"Now, all ready to hear the speech!"
"Specch! Speech!" cried the Thimble People.
Sewing Bird began:

"Our Mistress dear,
Your heart to cheer,
We're going to give a party;
And we will evermore be true,
And everyone of us to you
Will pledge allegiance hearty."

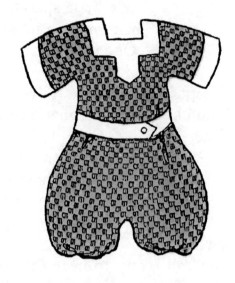

14. Rompers

 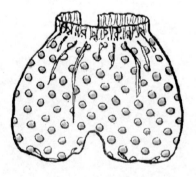

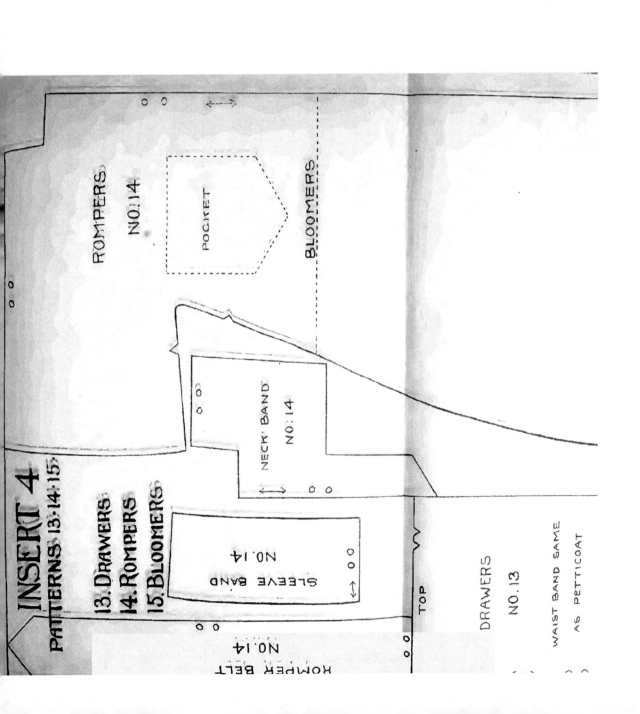

INSERT 4
PATTERNS 13·14·15

13. DRAWERS
14. ROMPERS
15. BLOOMERS

ROMPERS
NO. 14

POCKET

BLOOMERS

NECK BAND
NO. 14

SLEEVE BAND
NO. 14

TOP

ROMPER BELT
NO. 14

DRAWERS
NO. 13

WAIST BAND SAME
AS PETTICOAT

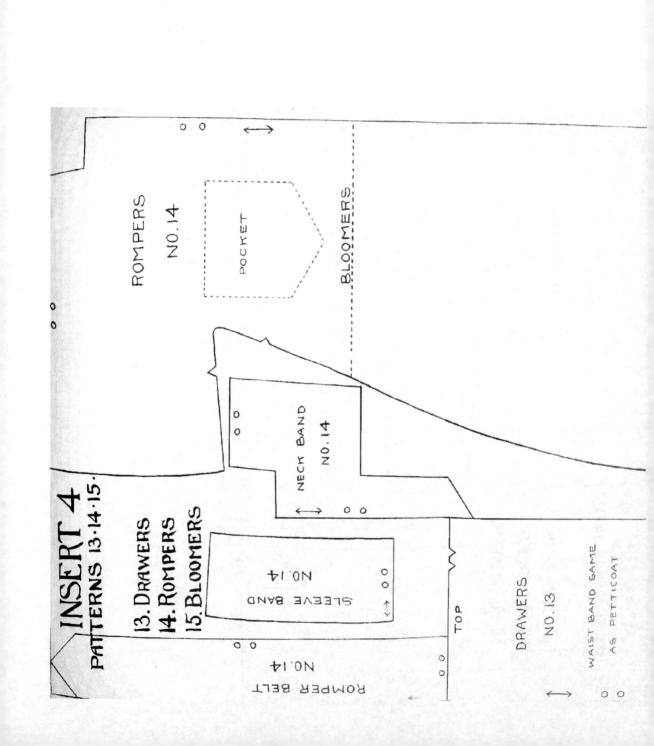

INSERT 4
PATTERNS 13·14·15·

13. DRAWERS
14. ROMPERS
15. BLOOMERS

ROMPERS
NO.14

POCKET

BLOOMERS

NECK BAND
NO.14

SLEEVE BAND
NO.14

ROMPER BELT
NO.14

TOP

DRAWERS
NO.13

WAIST BAND SAME
AS PETTICOAT

"Next—"
Then came Silver Thimble, bowing before Sewing
Bird,

"I'm Silver Thimble,
Bright and nimble."

Then Scissors Shears, bowing,

"I'm Scissors Shears,
With rather long ears."

"I'm Scissors Shears"

Then Tommy Pin Cushion,

"I'm Tomato Pin Cushion—
(Silv, stop your pushin'!)"

Then Emery Bag,

"I'm Emery Bag,
I never brag."

"I'm Tomato Pin Cushion"

Then Needle Book,

> "I'm Needle Book,
>   Please take a look,
>   And do not look awry;
>   I hold within
>   Without a pin,
>   The Needle-of-Don't-Have-to-Try."

Then Pen Cil,

> "I always do right."

"That's no rhyme!" exclaimed Scissors Shears.
"Well, it sounds better than

> "I'm Pen Cil,
>   I present my bill.

"Now," said Sewing Bird,

> "The little Tom Thumb Folks
>   Will all together bow—"

"Bow, wow, wow!" finished Tommy Pin Cushion, and all the Thimble People laughed. Their laughing sounded as if the button box had been upset.

Then the needles and pins and buttons began to bow and dance, making such a funny sight that Mary Frances nearly laughed aloud.

"Won't our mistress be pleased with all of us!" exclaimed Tommy Pin Cushion. "Come, pets!" and the needles and pins flew to him.

"Come, pets!" mimicked Emery Bag, and a few needles left Tommy Pin Cushion to go to him.

"Piggy!" exclaimed Emery Bag, looking crossly at Tommy Pin Cushion.

"Oh, no," said Tommy. "I'm just softer-hearted than you,—so they cling to me."

"Tee-hee," laughed Silver Thimble; "but—our little Miss will be pleased with this party, for—

"We're all here,
   We're all here;
Ready to see
   Our Mistress dear."

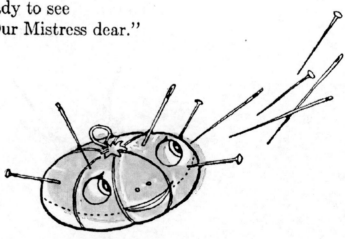

"Come, pets!"

Then came a whirring sound,

> "Zee-zee-zee-zee
>   Zumm, zumm, zumm,
>   Zumm, zumm, zumm,
>   Zee-zumm, zee-zumm,
>   Zee-zumm, zee-zumm-m-m"

and Mary Frances noticed the Sewing Machine wheels going around.

"Oh, my! Oh, my!" exclaimed Sewing Bird, fluttering her wings and tugging to get away from the table,

> "What an awful mistake,
>   No song I can make—
>   We forgot Ma!"

Oh, my!
Oh, my!

"Forgot whom?" asked Tommy Pin Cushion.

"Forgot me," zummed Sewing Machine. "All theze dayz, my little onez, I've been hearing theze lovely lezzons—but not one of you, no, not one, remembered your Ma Chine! Zum! Zum!"

"Zee-zumm, zee-zumm-m-m"

"What shall we do?" whispered the Thimble People.

> "Listen to what
>   I zay, I zay!
> I will take part
>   To-day, to-day!"

> "I cannot bear
>   A thing like thiz,
> I wished to help
>   Our little Mizz,
> Zumm! Zumm!"

Then all the Thimble People cried together,

> "Oh, Miss Ma Chine,
>   Oh, our Ma Chine,
> Forgive us all—
>   Don't make a scene!"

"Zum! Zeee-zeum," began Ma Chine, when Mary Frances stepped in the door.

"Magic and Mystery," she said, smiling. "I heard it all—all the lovely Presentation Party   I

couldn't bear to interrupt it—and I do thank you every one, my dear little friends—and my new friend, Ma Chine."

"Zum-zum," hummed Sewing Machine softly

"Some day," added Mary Frances, "when we have time, we will have the Grand Presentation Party all over again."

"Oh, goody! goody! won't it be grand!" cried the Thimble People.

"To-day's lesson," began Fairy Lady, "is to make a kimono for Mary Marie."

Mary Frances gravely sat Mary Marie in a chair and opened her trunk.

"That Japanese crepe is just right for the purpose," said Fairy Lady, "with this plain lavender three-quarter inch ribbon for trimming."

"Oh goody! goody!"

"Now comes

PATTERN 6.—DOLL'S KIMONO

See Insert I

1. Cut out by pattern of bath robe.
2. Clip several little gashes in the edge of the neck, and turn fronts and neck back on right side of goods one-quarter of an inch. Crease flat.

Clip several gashes in neck

Do the same to the ends of the sleeves.

3. Lay three-quarter inch ribbon flat on top of the turned edges of the kimono. Baste.

To fit ribbon around curves, gather it along the fuller edge.

4. Overhand, run, or stitch down the edges along the front opening of kimono and sleeves.

5. Hem, run, or stitch down the opposite edge of the ribbon.

6. Baste seams of kimono together on right side.

Try on. Make French seams.

7. Finish the bottom of kimono with a three-quarter inch hem.

NOTE.—Instead of ribbon, trimming bands of plain lawn may be used. If these are used, proceed in the following manner:

For neck and fronts, cut band exactly the same shape as the opening of kimono, making the band one and a half inches wide.

Cut two sleeve bands each seven inches long and two inches wide.

After turning in the edges of kimono opening, turn in the edges of the trimming band one-quarter inch.

Lay it against kimono opening, fitting the neck carefully.

Fold sleeve bands in half, lengthwise. Crease well.

Open. Pin band flat against end of sleeve. Stitch one-quarter inch from edge. Turn over and crease. Turn down the other side of band one-quarter inch. Fold band along the center crease. Bring turned-in edge of band over the edge stitched to sleeve.

Pin band to bottom of sleeve

Baste. Hem or stitch down.

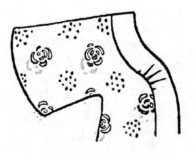

Fit ribbon around curves

Fairy Lady gave these directions very slowly, and Mary Frances followed them carefully. When she came to stitching the band, Sewing Ma Chine said,

"Little Lady Seamstress, please just put that under my foot, and it will be done in nearly no time."

"Thank you, Ma Chine, but Mother wouldn't let me," said Mary Frances.

"Oh, I'll be responsible!" said Ma Chine, and as Mary Frances set the little sleeve under the foot, she began to whirl her wheels so rapidly, Mary Frances couldn't see them.

"Oh, thank you," said the little girl. "Will you do the front trimming band?"

"Yez, indeed," said Ma Chine, singing "Zum-zum-zum!"

"Isn't this delightful, Mary Marie!" exclaimed the little girl. "What a lot of dear friends we have!"

Then Fairy Lady smiled. "The next is

PATTERN 7.—DRESSING SACK

See Insert I

1. Cut out by pattern of bath robe, making it only as long as the row of pinholes marked Dressing Sack.

"I'll be responsible"

2. Finish the fronts and neck, and sleeves by "pinking," or notching closely with the scissors; or,

3. Transfer the pattern for scallops given below.

To do this—With a soft lead pencil, trace scallops through the tissue paper.

Turn the tissue over, and lay the picture of scallops against the sleeves (and fronts), and trace over on the wrong side.

This will leave a penciled outline on the goods.

Instead of this method, the outline of the scallops may be traced through tissue and "carbon" paper.

With embroidery cotton, work the scallops in blanket stitch.

THE DRESSING SACK MAY BE FINISHED WITH RIBBON OR BANDS, in just the same way as the kimono. Embroider the ribbon or bands with

31.—FEATHER STITCHING

To learn to make the stitch, use linen canvas 3 in. by 7 in., and blunt needle and heavy red working cotton.

1. Work toward you. Hold canvas over the left forefinger.

2. Five threads in and down at left hand corner, draw needle through from underneath. Let thread hang.

3. Count one thread to right, point needle downward slanting to hole directly beneath the hole needle first came through. Pull through.

4. Repeat, inserting needle one hole to the left instead of right. Always let thread fall under point of needle on right side of canvas, before pulling it through.

Feather
Stitching

Transfer pattern for scallops

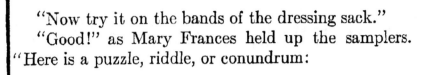

"Now try it on the bands of the dressing sack."

"Good!" as Mary Frances held up the samplers. "Here is a puzzle, riddle, or conundrum:

> "Mary Marie is feather-stitched—
> Yet not a feather is on her."

Mary Frances laughed. "I wonder how she'd look in feathers," she said—
Then Sewing Bird sang:

> "She'd make a fine bird,
> Upon my word,
> She'd sing a sweet song,
> And the only thing wrong—
> Her feathers and song
> Would be tightly glued on!"

"Oh, Sewing Bird!" laughed Mary Frances, shaking her finger, "how did you know the voice of a 'talking doll' was 'glued on'?"

How did you know the voice of a 'talking doll' was 'glued on'?

CHAPTER XXI

AUNT MARIA MAKES A VISIT

"NOW, one thing more,—
A pinafore,
We'll make for a doll
We almost adore."

A pinafore

"A pinafore!—Sewing Bird Lady," exclaimed Mary Frances. "An apron for Mary Marie?"

"Yes," smiled Fairy Lady, "a big apron which she can use as a dress until you make her some dresses—then she can use it as a 'cover-me-up' apron."

"Oh, good!" said Mary Frances, "and, dear Fairy Lady, I want to tell you—I've a lovely surprise! My Aunt Maria is coming to see us."

"Aunt Maria—oh, does she love sewing?"

"Indeed she does! She made a bed quilt when she was—let me see,—maybe—I think—it was when she was two years old."

"Tee-hee!" giggled Tommy Pin Cushion.

"Oh, I beg your pardon," he said, pretending he had stepped on Scissors Shears' toes.

"A-choooo!" said Needle Book, pretending to sneeze.

"She must have been a wonderful child," said Fairy Lady.

"She was," said Mary Frances, "and the loveliest cook ever! She told me all about it! She almost knew the Kitchen People."

"Well, I'm glad such a delightful person is coming, I'm sure," said Fairy Lady, "but let us have as much done as possible before she gets here. To do to-day's lesson, we have to learn the best way for

32.—SEWING ON BUTTONS

1. Make a pinhole where the button is to be sewed. Thread a No. 7 needle with No. 36 cotton—the cotton double,—and make a knot.

2. From the right side put needle down through the cloth in the pinhole mark, bringing the knot on the right side. The knot is then hidden under the button.

3. Bring the needle partly through near the knot on the right side.

4. Put the button on needle. Draw needle through.

5. Take a stitch down through the opposite hole, and put a pin through this stitch.

6. Sew through the holes, making a cross over the button and pin.

7. Take out the pin.   This will loosen the stitches.

8. Bring out the needle from under side of cloth, between the button and cloth.

9. Wind the thread around the stitches under the button three or four times.   This allows for the thickness of the button hole.

10. Fasten on the wrong side.

In sewing a button with a shank or loop, take several over and over stitches with double thread.

If putting on a number of buttons, the button-holes should be made first, and the place for buttons be marked through them.

"When does Aunt Maria arrive?" asked Fairy Lady.

"I don't exactly know," said Mary Frances.

"Oh, I hope—" began Scissors Shears;—then the bell rang.

"A lady to see you, Miss," said Katie, coming up-stairs.

"It's Aunt Maria!   It's Aunt Maria!" exclaimed Mary Frances, jumping down the stairs, two steps at a time.

"Oh, dear Aunt Maria, how perfectly grand!" kissing the old lady again and again.   "Have you had

"A lady to see you Miss"

Wind thread around stitches

lunch?   Grandma always takes an outing on Wednesday afternoons, and she'll be so sorry not to be home to welcome you!"

"But I feel very welcome," laughed Aunt Maria, "and I have had lunch, thank you, my dear."

"Then you can come right up-stairs," said Mary Frances, leading the way to the guest-room.

After taking off her hat and smoothing her hair, Aunt Maria began:

"ome
ght
p-stairs"

"What are you doing, child, all alone this afternoon —are you often alone?   You have no chance to cook here, I imagine."

"No, Aunt Maria," said Mary Frances.   "I'm very busy, never-the-less."

"Busy!" exclaimed Aunt Maria; "and what do you do, pray?"

"S'sh! Aunt Maria—it's another secret!"

"How lovely!" smiled the old lady

"I'm—" standing on tip-toe to whisper into her aunt's ear—"I'm learning to sew."

"No?" exclaimed Aunt Maria. "Why, my dear child, how—how can you learn to sew? I know your grandma cannot see to teach you—her eyes are too weak."

"I feel very welcome"

"Aunt Maria," whispered Mary Frances, "I've some little friends who know all about sewing, who teach me how—but it's a 'dead secret,' and you must never, never, never tell—hope you'll die if you do—will you promise—skull and cross-bones?"

"Mercy! Child!" exclaimed the old lady, "what an awful vow! But I'll not tell, and if I give my word—"

"Oh, I am sure you won't, Aunt Maria,—and—some day I'll be able to tell you *all* about it."

"Is it a book—like the cooking lessons,—that delightful secret? I won't tell."

"My!" thought Mary Frances. "Wouldn't Sauce Pan laugh!"

"Not exactly like that," said Mary Frances aloud, "and I know you'll never-never tell, Aunt Maria,—but it's a very-very serious secret, for nobody knows—not even Mother."

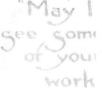

"May I see some of your work, my dear?"

"I'll bring some to show you," she said. "Excuse me, please."

She stood on the threshold of the sewing room a moment before entering. All the Thimble People were jumping around in excitement.

"I tell you," tinkled Silver Thimble, "it's the Aunt!"

"It's not!" piped the thinnest little voice Mary Frances had ever heard.

"Hello!" exclaimed Scissors Shears. "That's little Common Ordinary Pin! You don't know! You haven't much of a head."

"Maybe not," answered the thin voice, "but we have some fine points."

"Ha! ha!" laughed Tommy Pin Cushion.

"And we're not stuck on ourselves!"

"Ha! ha!" laughed Tommy Pin Cushion again.

"No," exclaimed Scissors Shears, "you're stuck on Tommy Pin Cushion—such taste!"

Mary Frances went into the room.

"Oh," said Fairy Lady, "I was afraid you might not be alone."

"Mary Frances!" came Aunt Maria's voice from nearby.

Every Thimble person fell down where he was, and in a twinkle Fair Lady became Sewing Bird.

"I thought I wouldn't trouble you to bring your work to me, so I've followed you to the sewing room,"

"I was afraid you might not be alone"

17. Fur Lined Cape

27. Rain Coat

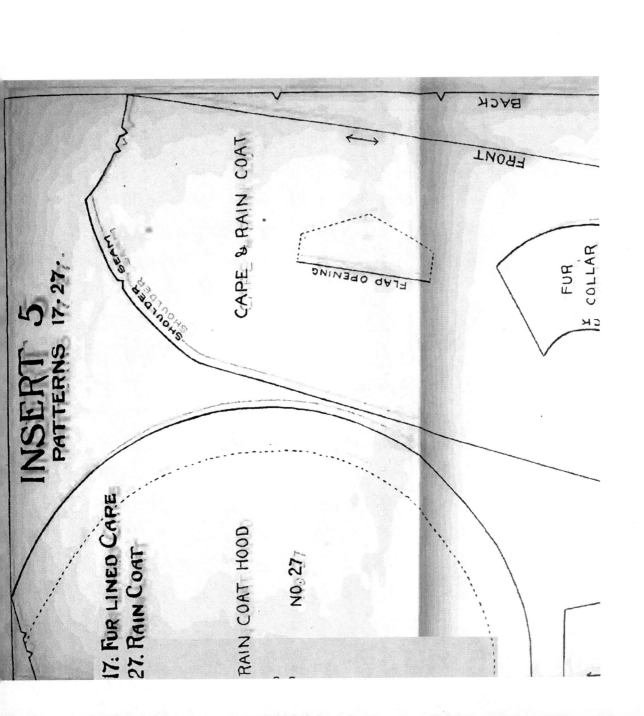

INSERT 5
PATTERNS 17·27·

17. FUR LINED CAPE
27. RAIN COAT

RAIN COAT HOOD

No. 27

SHOULDER SEAM

CAPE & RAIN COAT

FLAP OPENING

BACK

FRONT

FUR
COLLAR

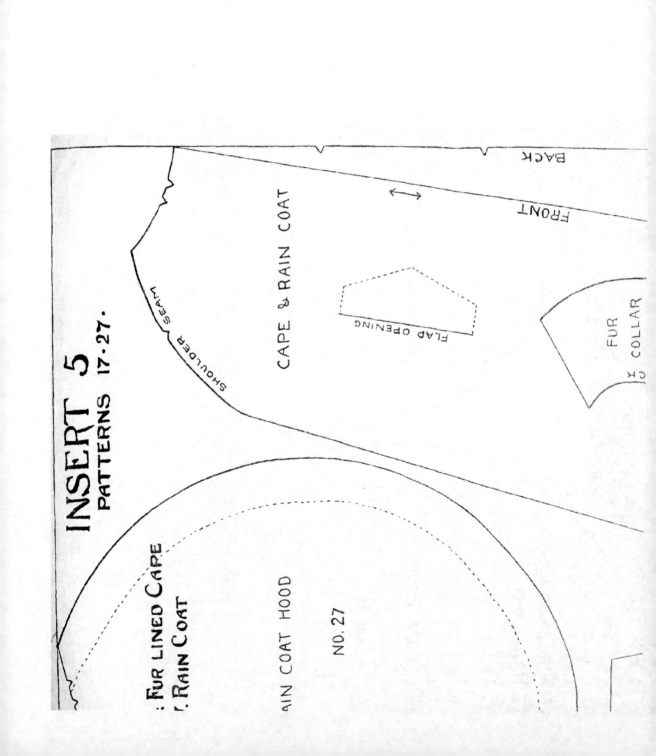

INSERT 5
PATTERNS 17·27.

FUR LINED CAPE
RAIN COAT

CAPE & RAIN COAT

SHOULDER SEAM

FLAP OPENING

FUR COLLAR

FRONT

BACK

RAIN COAT HOOD

NO. 27

said the old lady, "I thought I heard—I'm quite certain I heard some one talking."

"Oh, my!" thought Mary Frances.

"Goodness!" exclaimed Aunt Maria as they went into the room. "Although I oughtn't to say it—what an untidy room! My dear child, my dear child, everything ought to be put in place just as soon as you've used it. It never pays to lay anything down out of place. Here are needles and pins, scissors and needle-book, emery bag, and what not—tumbled over the table, and the work basket on its side! You'll learn better, though, child."

There was a strange expression on the little girl's face.

"It's rude, Mary Frances, to smile when you're in fault," continued the old lady.

Goodness

"Excuse me, Aunt Maria," said Mary Frances. "I couldn't help it."

"Well, I expect it's because you're so glad to see me," said Aunt Maria, leaning back in her chair and rocking.

"Never mind, we'll look at your work. Very creditable, very creditable indeed, child! Such excellent

Work basket on its side

stitches,'' examining the little samplers, and finally the bath robe and kimono. "You certainly do take after me. To think that so spoiled a child should develop into such an excellent character! 'Blood will tell!' I've often said it—'Blood will tell!' What pretty material! By the way, child, where do you get the goods—if this is a secret?''

"Oh, Aunt Maria!"

"Oh, Aunt Maria, Mother sent me this little trunk full of these pretty things; and this lovely, lovely doll, Mary Marie, to amuse myself with. She said she was so sorry not to be able to show me how to sew, and hopes to, when she comes home. Dear Mother! Won't she be surprised?''

"Indeed she will," said the old lady, examining the contents of the trunk. "But," she sniffed, "I am compelled to say less beautiful goods would have answered the purpose. When I was a little girl—well, never mind! Have you learned to make button-holes?''

"I can make the stitch, I think," answered Mary Frances, meekly.

"Well, I'll teach you, child," said Aunt Maria, getting a piece of muslin ready. "Now, let us begin to learn how to make

"Indeed she will"

33.—BUTTON-HOLES

All button-holes should be worked in a double fold of cloth. Use for practice, a piece of muslin six inches long and four inches wide. Fold through the center. Turn in and baste along edges.

(A) *To Cut*

With button-hole scissors, cut into the goods one quarter of an inch from folded edge. Cut along a thread of the goods to make it straight. Make opening a little longer than the button is broad. For button-hole, use No. 40 cotton, No. 8 needle. Barring and overcasting are often done with a finer thread than that used for the button-holing.

(B) *To Bar*

1. Make a small knot in thread.
2. Put the goods over first finger, left hand — folded edge toward you.
3. At the end of button-hole farthest from folded edge of cloth, insert needle between the double cloth, bringing it out at A. (See picture.)
4. Point needle down at B; bring it out at A.
5. Point needle down at C; bring it out at D. Do this twice.
6. Point needle down at B; bring it out at A.

(C) *Overcasting*

Overcast the edge on each side and end of the button-hole, catching the long "barring" threads.

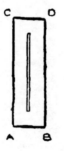

To Bar   Overcasting

(D) *Button-hole Stitch*

1. With goods over forefinger of left hand, at end of button-hole farthest from the folded edge of the cloth, insert needle between the muslin; pull through, leaving a small end of thread between muslin.

2. At same corner of button-hole, bring needle half way through. Taking both threads hanging from eye of needle between thumb and finger of right hand, pass the thread *under* the point of the needle, from right to left. Pull needle through, drawing the thread firmly near the button-hole. This forms the purl, which is well adapted to the constant wear upon the button-hole.

3. Repeat until needle is at first stitch taken.

(E) *Finishing*

1. Make barring stitches over the first barring stitches taken.

Button-hole stitch

2. Put needle through these barring stitches, forming the blanket or loop stitch,—make several loop stitches and bring needle to wrong side.

3. Fasten thread by several small stitches.

Note.—If thread is too short to finish button-holing, fasten it on wrong side of material. Enter the new thread on wrong side and bring thread through last button-hole purl, or twisted edge.

Aunt Maria gave Mary Frances these directions very slowly, making the little girl do each step as she explained.

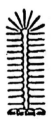

Finished button-hole

"No, not that way, child," she would say. "Sit up straight; place both feet firmly on the floor; hold your sewing high; do not stoop over. That is the correct position while sewing. Throw the thread more carefully. No, not so long a thread—it will tangle. Patience—child!"

"My," exclaimed Mary Frances, "that's the hardest thing I've done yet. Am I very trying to teach?"

"Well," said the old lady, "you might be more so—but that's a real respectable button-hole. But really, child, I must again repeat my lesson to you about neatness. Never leave your sewing room as I found it to-day."

"There's Grandma!" exclaimed Mary Frances, looking out the window. "Come, Aunt Maria, let's go down."

"Is my necktie straight?" asked the old lady of Mary Frances, taking her hand.

"My, that's the hardest thing yet"

. . . .

"My," said Mary Frances, returning to the sewing room, "aren't they the dear old dears, talking

"Is my necktie straight?"

together!   A cup of tea and those two old ladies—
there's nothing under the sun they can't think of—
from Noah-and-the-ark to Forever-more!   I wonder
if I can finish Mary Marie's pinafore.   I'm going to
make Angie a lot of clothes like Mary Marie's."

"Will the Old Grunt be back?"   Scissors Shears
was looking up at Mary Frances.

"Who?" asked Mary Frances.

"She is an old Grunt!"

"The Old Grunt," said Scissors Shears, "fussin'
and gruntin' over everything.   We looked all right.
She scared us—if we hadn't dropped where we were
she might have found out about us—and if she'd found
out about us—we'd been Never-Nevers."

'You must not call names," said Mary Frances,
gravely.

"She is an Old Grunt! So there! It was my work
to teach you to make button-holes, and I so wanted
to do it!" burst out Button-hole Scissors, excitedly.

He spread his funny little legs apart and looked up
at Mary Frances most forlornly.

"Rip-her-up-the-back! Butty," growled Scissors
Shears.

"Be quiet!" exclaimed Mary Frances, "I'm

"It was my work to teach you!"

ashamed of you both!   I know it's an awful disappointment to you, Button-hole Scissors, but, never mind, you shall help me sometime.''

"Magic and Mystery, we must—"

"Yes," said Fairy Lady, smiling, "we must finish the pinafore.   Here is

PATTERN 8.—DOLL'S PINAFORE
See Insert II

To cut out—

1. Fold goods lengthwise.   Place edge of pattern having two rings (oo) on this fold.   Pin in place.   Cut out.

2. Indicate place for straps and pocket by pricking with a pin, through pattern and material.   Remove pattern.

Run a red basting thread through the pinholes.

3. Cut four straps, and the pocket.

To make—

NOTE.—The pinafore is not joined under the arms; therefore,

1. Make a narrow hem along the sides of the front and back.

2. Make a three-quarter inch hem along the bottom of pinafore.

3. Make a tiny clip in the corners of the neck opening.

Turn down one-quarter inch along neck on right side.

4. Baste flat against this, one-half inch wide white linen tape. In turning corners, turn the tape completely over.

5. Ends of sleeves, sides of sleeves, and sides and bottom of pinafore finished in same way.

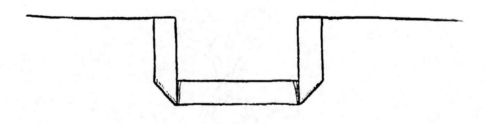

Pocket

1. Make a quarter-inch hem at top of pocket.
2. Turn in edges one-eighth inch.   Baste.
3. Pin in place shown on pattern.   Hem, or stitch.

Straps

1. Turn in edges of straps one-eighth inch all around.

2. Baste two straps together, wrong sides facing each other.

Overhand, or stitch together.

4. Pin in place as shown by red basting thread, and sew in place through a button.

Or, a button may be sewed to the pinafore, and a button-hole worked in each end of the straps.

(If this is done, hem a small piece of goods on the wrong side of pinafore under the places for the buttons, so that the pulling of the button will not tear the goods.)

Pin in place

"And we'll all help,—if you please."

"Thank you, dear Thimble People," said Mary Frances, spreading the pretty gingham on the sewing table.   "Work very quickly—I haven't many minutes. I'm so tired, anyhow," and she leaned back in her rocking chair.

Sew strap in place

"Mary Frances, Mary Frances, Mary Frances, dear!" called Grandma's voice.

"Oh," thought Mary Frances, "I've been asleep. It's twilight, nearly."

"Yes, Grandma," she called. "I'll come right down." And she looked on the table expecting to see the gingham spread out, but it was nowhere to be seen.

"Look at Mary Marie," whispered Sewing Bird.

There sat the proud dolly with the gingham pinafore all made and buttoned in place.

"How,—how?" stammered Mary Frances.

> "We took her over
>   To Thimble Land;
>   Over to our
>   Fairyland,"

explained Sewing Bird.

"Can I go there some day?" asked Mary Frances.

> "I think you may,
>   But not to-day;

Perhaps you'll go
Another day!"

sang Sewing Bird.

"Oh, thank you, you dear!" said Mary Frances.

"Come, Mary Frances," again called Grandma.
"Why, dear child," she said, kissing the little girl,
"it's nearly six o'clock, and we old ladies have been so
busy living in the past that we almost forgot the present
—that's you."

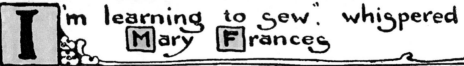

I'm learning to sew", whispered Mary Frances

CHAPTER XXII

A RUINED DRESS

"SO the Old Grunt had to go home," said Scissors Shears, standing on one pointed toe.

"Why?" asked Tommy Pin Cushion.

"I don't care a tinkle," exclaimed Silver Thimble, "why she went—I'm only glad we're to have the little Miss to ourselves once more!"

"Humph!" exclaimed Ma Chine, "if Sewing Bird were awake, little you'd speak in so cutting a way about an old lady, Scissors!"

"Click! Click! Clickety-click! Rip-her-up-the-back!" snapped Scissors Shears, making across the table.

"You old Thread Chewer, you!" he exclaimed, "everybody knows you have wheels in your head! You old Thread Chewer! You—! You! I double dare you to—"

"Zumm! Zumm! Zumm!" Ma Chine began to whirl.

"Oh, what are the comical things going to do," thought Mary Frances at the door. "I do hope **no** harm will be done! I'll wait a minute and see."

[175]

"I dont care a tinkle"

Suddenly Scissors Shears stumbled and fell flat on the table, his feet being all entangled in the folds of some pink lawn.

"Zumm! Zumm!" whirled Ma Chine. "Why don't you come? Come on, Sweet-tempered!"

"Oh, my!" moaned Scissors Shears. "Oh, me! I'm almost undone!"

"Undone!" exclaimed Sewing Bird. "I think you're done-up,—

"Oh, my!
Oh, me!"

"Oh, how it shames
 To call bad names!
 And temper lost
 Makes heavy cost!"

"Sewing Bird, that's true!" exclaimed Scissors Shears, getting up, "Oh, the dear little Miss! Oh, what a lesson! I'm so sorry I lost my temper!"

"What can he have done?" thought Mary Frances, peeping in the door.

There on the sewing table was Scissors Shears looking woefully upon a pretty little doll's dress carefully cut out and pinned together. All over it were

All over it were dashes

gashes and slashes where his sharp feet had cut into the material.

"What shall I do," began Scissors Shears, "oh, Sewing Bird, what shall I do?—There's no other goods! I took such care to make that so perfect,—ready for the little lady's lesson to-day!"

"Come!" said Mary Frances to herself. "That's enough! Poor old Scissors Shears!—I'll pretend not to notice it.

Good-afternoon!" she said going into the sewing room, "I've changed my mind, dear Sewing Bird Lady—I think I'd like to use some other goods rather than that I left on the table for this lesson. I'll just throw this aside in a little bundle,"—pushing the ruined dress aside,—"and may I use this pretty pink chambray gingham to-day?"

"The very thing!" exclaimed Fairy Lady, "much better than lawn, for a morning dress; and here is

"Good afternoon" she said

PATTERN 9.—DOLL'S MORNING DRESS
See Insert II

1. Cut out in same way as pinafore.
2. For neck-band, use a six-inch square of white lawn.

"The very thing!"

Fold through the center.   Fold again through the center.

3. Place neck-band pattern on the lawn, having the edges which are marked with two rings (oo) each on a fold.

4. Pin in place.   Cut out.   Open.   Make tiny clip in each corner of the neck opening.

5. Cut sleeve-bands of white lawn, with double rings (oo) on fold of cloth.

To make—

1. Turn over opening of neck of dress one-eighth inch on right side.   Crease, without stretching.   Baste.

2. Turn both edges of neck-band down one-eighth inch, on same side of goods.   Crease, without stretching.

3. Spread the dress open on the table.

Lay neck-band with turned-in edge against turned-in edge of dress neck.   Pin in place.   Baste.

Stitch; or, overhand and hem, in place.

4. Turn up ends of sleeves, and sew sleeve-bands in place in the same way.

5. Make placket by directions given on next page.

Make three button-holes on right hand side.   Sew three buttons on left hand side.

6. Join under-arms with French seams.

7. Make a three-quarter inch hem in bottom of dress.

"I'll cut that out quickly," said Mary Frances, pinning the pattern on the goods.

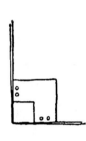

Edges
marked oo
each on
fold

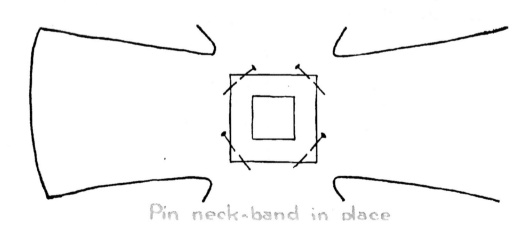

Pin neck-band in place

"Mark the place where the pocket goes," said Fairy Lady.

"Why," she exclaimed at length, holding up the little dress, "the back is just like the front, and the neck is too little for her head to slip through."

"Exactly!" smiled Fairy Lady looking pleased. "You are very observant."

"That's a lovely word!" thought Mary Frances. "I'll remember it."

"You may now fold the dress lengthwise, and from the neck, cut down the middle of the back four inches, which will make the opening large enough for her head —and learn about

The back is just like the front

34.—MAKING A PLACKET,

which is the finished opening of a dress or skirt.

1. Cut one piece of cloth like the dress—two inches wide, and as long as the dress opening.

2. Cut another piece one inch wide and as long as the opening. Fold in half the long way, and crease.

3. On the right hand side of the opening, face the raw edge back on the wrong side with the narrow piece of cloth.

4. On the left hand side, sew the wider piece of cloth, as if for facing,—but after turning in the edge, fold on the creased middle fold, bringing edge exactly over the first sewing.

Extension Placket

This is an Extension Placket.

This piece can be used without folding: then the edge must be hemmed.

There should be two rows of stitching across the bottom of the placket to strengthen it

On this page are pictures of two other kinds of placket.

To make a Hemmed Placket, sew a narrow hem on left side, and broad hem on right hand side. Fold broad hem over narrow, and stitch in place across lower end.

A Tape Placket is very useful in making petticoats. Face the opening with flat tape.

Fairy Lady handed Mary Frances a sheet of paper.

"Where did this come from?" asked Mary Frances.

"It's a fairy paper," answered Fairy Lady. "That's all I can tell."

'It is beautiful!" said Mary Frances, holding the picture of the plackets in her hand, "Thank you."

"Can you tell me what to do next?" asked Fairy Lady.

"Yes," answered Mary Frances, "I must work in this order in making my dolly's dresses:

Hemmed Placket

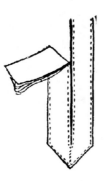

Tape Placket.

Tape folded

18. Afternoon Dress

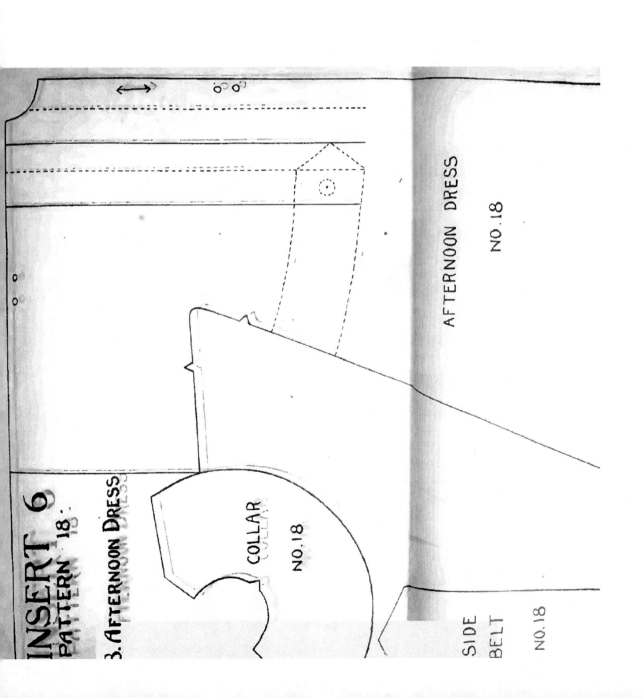

INSERT 6
PATTERN 18.

3. AFTERNOON DRESS

COLLAR
NO.18

AFTERNOON DRESS
NO.18

SIDE
BELT
NO.18

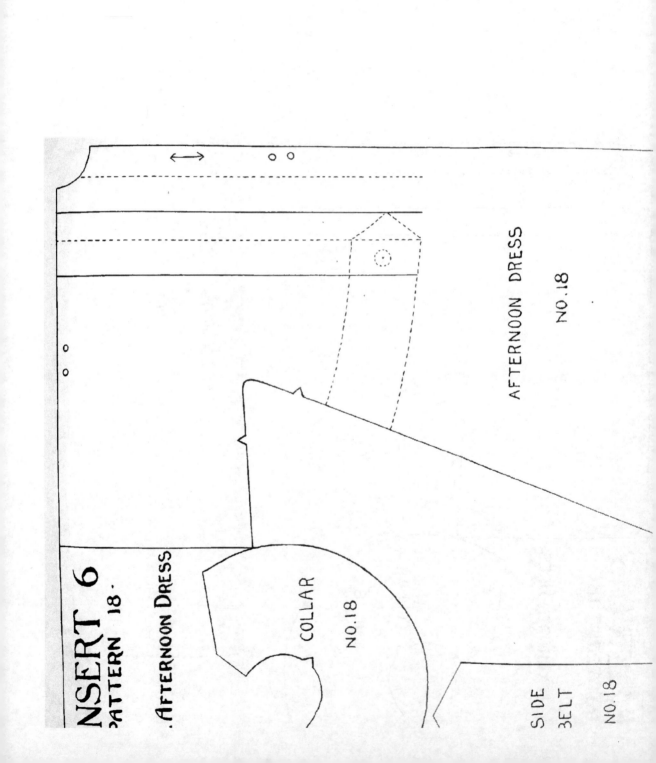

INSERT 6

PATTERN 18

AFTERNOON DRESS

AFTERNOON DRESS

NO.18

COLLAR

NO.18

SIDE
BELT

NO.18

1. Basting of seams.
2. Fitting.
3. Altering, if necessary.
4. Sewing seams.
5. Facing the neck with the fitted facing.—Baste that on wrong side; then turn to the right side; turn in, and hem down.
6. Facings on the sleeves in same way.
7. Pocket hemmed at top. Turned in, and basted in place; stitched in place.
8. Buttons and button-holes.

"That's your week's work," said Fairy Lady, "if you finish it for the next lesson, I'll be so proud."

"And so will I!" laughed Mary Frances, resolving to work hard. "Good-day, dear Thimble People."

.   .   .   .

"I'll help her if I dare," said Scissors Shears.

"What could you do, now?" asked Tommy Pin Cushion. "You're in disgrace!"

"He could only undo," said Needle Book.

"That will do!" said Sewing Bird.

"What shall I do?" began Scissors Shears

CHAPTER XXIII
THE FLANNEL PET

"DON'T you want to go with Grandma to-day?" asked her grandmother of Mary Frances. "Where, Nanny?" inquired the little girl.

"Well," said Grandma, "I'm going to take a trolley ride through the park."

"Where the monkeys are?" inquired Mary Frances.

"Yes," said Grandma. "I thought you'd like to share my 'afternoon out.'"

"I dearly love monkeys"

"I dearly love monkeys," said Mary Frances. "They crinkle up their faces so!"

"Come, then," said Grandma, "get your hat!"

Mary Frances ran up-stairs. This is what she heard:

"I do hope the little lady will have it finished!"

"What does she make to-day?"

"The flannel pet—"

"Oh, good!"

[182]

"That's Silver Thimble," thought Mary Frances.

"Why do you say 'Oh, good'?" asked Scissors Shears.

"Because," answered Silver Thimble, "I know what fun she'll have. I feel closer to my little Miss than any of you others can."

"Ha!" laughed Tommy Pin Cushion, "but not love her better."

"The dear things!" thought Mary Frances, "and I was going to run away! What can a flannel pet be? Is it a flannel cat, or rabbit, or dog?"

"Mary Frances!" called Grandma.

"Listen, Nanny," said the little girl leaning over the banister, "will you feel much disappointed, dear Nanny, if I don't go? I— I—"

"Why, no, my child!" said Grandma. Mrs. Bennett is going with me, so I'll have company, but I thought you'd be lonely. Good-bye, dear,—take a nap if you feel like it."

"Good-bye, Nanny dear," smiled Mary Frances, throwing the old lady a kiss. "She really does spoil me, I fear," she thought. "I never had my own way so exactly before."

She dressed Mary Marie in the new morning dress.

"I certainly wish she had some petticoats," thought the little girl, taking her into the sewing room.

> "Oh, what fun!
> I see it's done!
> Quite in distress,
> Without this dress,
> Would be, you see,
> Our Sweet Marie,"

sang Sewing Bird, admiring the morning dress.

"But the button-holes," said Mary Frances, "are pretty poor, I must say!"

"That's because the Old Grunt taught you—" began Scissors Shears.

"Oh, my!" exclaimed Mary Frances.

"I forgot! I forgot!" said Scissors Shears. "I did, really and truly! your Seamstress-ship. Will you please forgive me?"

> "Scissors and Shears
> Now, change your ears,"

She dressed Mary Marie

"I wish she had some petticoats"

laughed Mary Frances, and the funny little long-eared fellow was on the table.

"I'm sure I'll not be able to use you to-day," said Mary Frances, "with those ears."

"You tell me what to do," said Scissors Shears, wagging his ears back and forward. "I like my ears. They do not help me work—but I can hear almost anything with them. I can hear what Tommy Pin Cushion is thinking."

"Goodness!" exclaimed Tommy Pin Cushion. "You must be most unhappy!"

Mary Frances laughed.

"What is to-day's lesson?" she asked.

Sewing Bird began to sing:

"I like my ears"

> "I see you haven't guessed it yet—
> It's just a little flannel pet.
> A period after pet. you'll note;
> It's short for flannel petticoat.
>> Oh, de de dum dum!
>> De-dee-dee!
>> No one could guess it—
>> That I see."

"Oh, Magic and Mystery," laughed Mary Frances, "Mary Marie will be delighted! She seems so chilly these days. I think she will soon be able to say a few words. I tried to think she said 'Ma-ma' to me to-day."

"It is lovely to help make things for so sweet a child," smiled Fairy Lady.

"That is a great compliment," said Mary Frances, "to her mother."

"It isn't only her lovely face," said Fairy Lady; "it's her charming manners."

"Oh, thank you!" said Mary Frances, "to a mother who tries to teach the best to her child, that is most pleasing to hear."

"There is even more in seeing her mother's manner than in teaching her, I think," said Fairy Lady.

Mary Frances blushed with pleasure.

"And now," said Fairy Lady, "ready for

"Oh, thank you!"

PATTERN 10.—DOLL'S FLANNEL PETTICOAT

Suggestions for material,—white woolen flannel.

1. Make a pattern of ordinary wrapping paper.

Use a ruler, making the pattern nine and one-half inches long, and five inches wide.

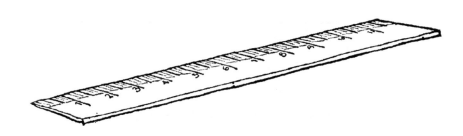

Use a ruler

2. Mark with two rings (oo) and an arrow (➤➤➤➤) as in picture.

To cut out—

1. Place end of pattern having two rings, on a lengthwise fold of material. Pin in place. Cut out.

To make—

(A) Leave one and one-half inches of the seam unsewed, for making of placket.

Below this, join seam by

35.—FELLING ON FLANNEL

A fell is a seam hemmed down to prevent edges from raveling.

NOTE.—To learn to make a fell, use two pieces of flannel, each six inches long, and three inches wide. Practise with these, before attempting the fell on the petticoat.

1. Place the pieces of flannel together, one edge extending one-eighth of an inch beyond the other.

2. Baste a narrow seam. Stitch.

3. Remove the bastings.

4. Turn to other side of goods. With a warm iron, press the seam with wider side covering the narrower. Do not open it.

In felling flannel, do not turn the wider part of the seam in, but leave it open, and baste down flat after pressing.

Catch-stitch it down instead of hemming.

(B) Make a Hemmed Placket.

Do not turn flannel twice; but, after pressing, catch-stitch down over the raw edges.

Felling on Flannel

To cut flannel petticoat pattern

(C) To Hem Petticoat.

1. Turn up one-quarter inch on wrong side, at bottom of skirt.
Baste, and press.
Remove bastings.

2. Turn up again on wrong side, three-quarters of an inch,
measuring and basting carefully. Press.

3. Feather-stitch in place along top of hem.
Remove bastings.

(D) Gather the top of petticoat.

1. Cut a notch in the middle of the front of petticoat.

2. Thread needle with No. 40 cotton. Use cotton double.
Gather petticoat at top, commencing at notch, gather first
in one direction, then in the other.

3. Leave knots in each end of the threads.
Make thread a little shorter than the length of the flannel.

NOTE.—This petticoat is not to be sewed to a band; but is
attached later, to Doll's Underwaist.

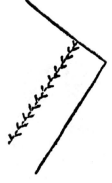

Feather stitch hem

Mary Frances had the Needle-of-Don't-Have-to-
Try in her hand, and soon finished the petticoat.

"Good!" exclaimed Fairy Lady. "Now comes

PATTERN 11.—DOLL'S UNDERWAIST

See Insert III

To cut out—

1. Pin pattern with arrow edge on a lengthwise fold of lawn.

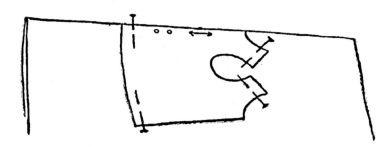

Pin on lengthwise fold of lawn

2. Cut two underwaists just alike.

3. Clip a small notch (V) in the exact center of the bottom of each waist.

To make—

1. Baste the shoulder seams of one waist together. (*a* to *a*; and *b* to *b*.)

Try on doll.

Alter if necessary.

2. Stitch one-quarter inch from the edge.

Open and flatten the seams.

3. Turn in edges along the back one-quarter inch. Baste.

Turn up bottom of waist one-quarter inch. Baste.

4. Clip several small gashes along the neck.

Turn in the edge of neck one-eighth of an inch. Baste.

Do the same to the armholes.

5. Do the same to the other waist.

6. Pin and baste the two waists together, wrong sides facing each other. Overhand (or stitch) all edges together, *except the bottom*, which is left open for the flannel petticoat.

Try on doll

7. To join flannel petticoat to underwaist—Insert gathers of petticoat between the two waists. Pin notches together, and baste in place. Hem down.

8. Sew three buttons on left side of back of waist: one at the neck, one in the center, one at the bottom. Make the button-holes on the other side of back of waist.

9. Sew one button at center front of waist, to fasten the lawn petticoat.

Overhand all edges together

"Scissors Shears, do your best," whispered Mary Frances, cutting into the muslin for the dolly's under-waist.

She felt Scissors Shears spring in her fingers.

"And now, not a word until it is finished!"

"What darlings!" she exclaimed, finally, holding up the little underwaist and flannel petticoat.

"Are they finished?" asked Fairy Lady, leaning forward in her rocking chair.

"Yes, all finished! If it hadn't been for the Needle-of-Don't-Have-to-Try, I'd have been a week doing them, I'm sure," said Mary Frances.

"I'll put them right on Mary Marie," she added, "she seems so cold."

"How must it be,
    How must it be,
To be beloved
    As well as she?"

sang Sewing Bird.

"You are, dear Sewing Bird," said Mary Frances. "Oh, dear little Sewing Bird, indeed, you are!"

Good!" exclaimed Fairy Lady

CHAPTER XXIV

THE WHITE PET

"WE'RE not through yet,—
    There's the white pet.
    Let's not forget—"

"Oh, I know what the white pet is, Sewing Bird," interrupted Emery Bag. "It's a white mouse! One of my uncles had a whole side eaten out of him by one of those sweet pets. I won't forget!"

    "Oh, my! oh, me!
      Let that be wrote,
  A *mouse* is not
    A petticoat!"

Sang
Sewing
Bird

sang Sewing Bird.

"Oh, you simple thing!" exclaimed Emery Bag. "Why didn't you say 'petticoat,' then?"

"One of my uncles had a side eaten out"

"If I take time
    To make a rhyme,
        A rhyme it then must be:
If words won't rhyme
    At any time—
        I cut them short, you see,"

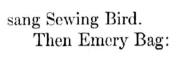

sang Sewing Bird.
    Then Emery Bag:

"If that is true
    Then this will do:
    To Sewing Bird
    Any old word
    Will make a rhyme,
    If shortened hyme.

Isn't that beautiful?"
    "What does 'hyme' mean?" cried Sewing Bird.
    "I haven't made up my mind, yet, what it means,"
said Emery Bag. "Sewing Bird, you've got an awfully
swelled head since—"
    "Nobody without a heart of steel would dare say

such things to Sewing Bird. Isn't he brave?" whispered Tommy Pin Cushion.

'A Brave's an Indian. I'm not an Indian!" retorted Emery Bag.

"Ready to fight any one!" said Tommy Pin Cushion.

"Reddy yourself!" exclaimed Emery Bag.

"Here!" exclaimed Scissors Shears. "Here is some muslin on the table. I'll cut out the white pet,—petty,—petticoat! That's parsed now, I guess!"

"It's not fit!" replied Emery Bag.

"It's not fight, you mean," interrupted Scissors Shears.

"It's not fitted, you mean," exclaimed Tommy Pin Cushion.

"It's not fit! I tell you!" again exclaimed Emery Bag.

"Well, Red-in-the-face—, Brave," interrupted Scissors Shears, "what's not fit?"

"It's all in the fit," sullenly muttered Emery Bag.

"How do you know?" exclaimed Tommy Pin Cushion. "Did you ever have a fit?"

"Of course, I have! Whenever I have my cover on!

"Redd yourself"

"Ready to fight anyone"

"Come what, come will,
    Then, this is it:
It is not fit
    To fit a fit;
If a fit fits you
    And you fit a fit,
Put it on
    As you would a mit:
Some say fight,
    But I say fit;
If you want to make sure,
    Come try it!
And this is double trouble—"

sang Emery Bag, bowing.

Everybody looked puzzled.

"It's plain he's in a fit," exclaimed Scissors Shears. "Rip-him-up-the-back!—If I don't get to work, there'll be no petticoat to fit on Mary Marie," and he dived into the muslin.

"Where's the pattern?" he asked, looking up. "Oh, where's the pattern, Sewing Bird?"

Then Sewing Bird began:

21. Coat (FRONT)

21. Coat (BACK)

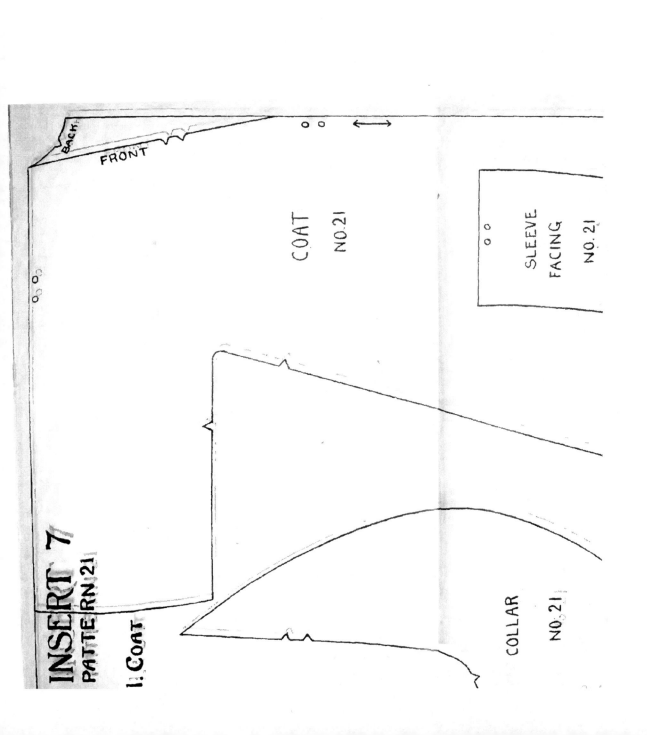

INSERT 7
PATTERN 21

1. Coat

BACK

FRONT

COAT
NO. 21

SLEEVE
FACING
NO. 21

COLLAR
NO. 21

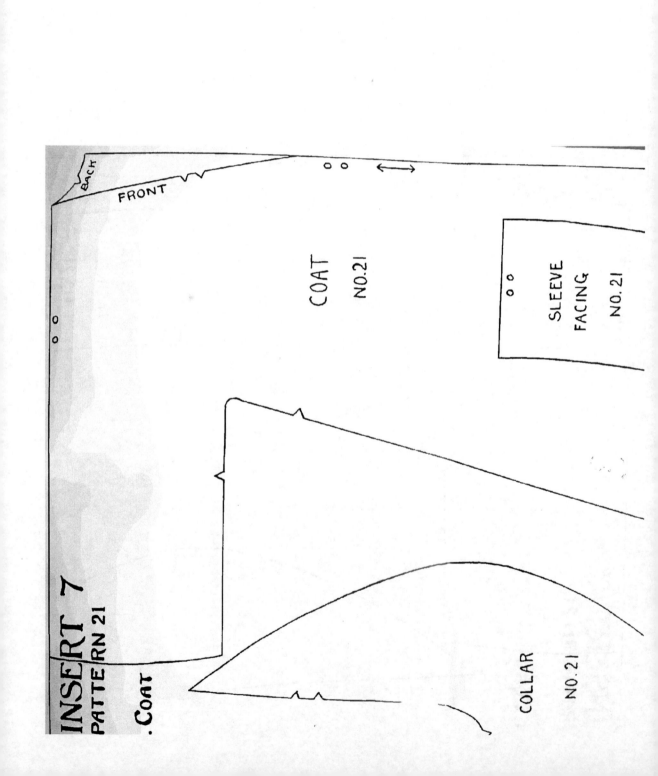

INSERT 7
PATTERN 21
.COAT

BACK

FRONT

COAT
NO.21

SLEEVE
FACING
NO. 21

COLLAR
NO.21

"Oh, woe, alas!
    Oh, woe is me!
Whenever they quarrel so,
    Can't you see—
Without this petty history—
    No pattern is for you or me,
Without 'Magic and Mystery!'
    Oh, woe! and more alases!"

"Magic and Mystery!" exclaimed Mary Frances standing in the doorway.

All the other Thimble People pretended to be asleep.

"Thank you, my dear!" exclaimed Sewing Bird Fairy Lady. "When they quarrel so, I cannot change from Sewing Bird into Fairy Lady without help,—but now,"—she added happily, "here is

Pattern 12.—Doll's Lawn Petticoat

1. Cut a pattern of ordinary wrapping paper, making it twelve inches long, and five and one-half inches wide.

2. Mark on one end, two rings (oo) and an arrow (➤➤—).

3. To mark tuck—

"Thank you, my dear!"

At one end, measure up two and one-half inches from bottom of pattern.   Mark with a dot.   Do same at other end.

Join these marks with a straight line.

Write along this line the word—TUCK.

One-quarter inch above this line, draw dotted line.

One-quarter inch below tuck line, draw dotted line.

To cut out—

1. Pin arrow end of pattern on a lengthwise fold of white dimity or lawn.   Cut out.

2. Marking tuck.—With a large pin, prick through pattern and lawn, along the tucking lines, making holes about half an inch apart; or, mark lines with a tracing wheel against a ruler.

3. Cut Band for Petticoat by Pattern 11.

See Insert III.

To make—

1. Join ends of petticoat with felled seam, making seam but three inches long, leaving it open above that, in order to make a placket.

2. In making a placket, use one-quarter of an inch hem on left hand side, and one-half an inch hem on right hand side.   Fold broad hem over narrow; secure at lower end with two rows of stitching.

3. Make the tuck.

Tracing wheel

36.—MAKING TUCKS

(*a*) Crease material back along the middle row of pinholes.

- -

TUCK
_____

- -

To mark tuck

(*b*) Stitch tuck on upper side, sewing through the other rows of pinholes.

NOTE.—In making several tucks, mark in the same way, and proceed in a like manner; but remember to cut the material sufficiently long to allow for the making.

4. Make a three-quarter inch hem at the bottom of petticoat.

5. Gather top in same way as flannel petticoat.

6. Set the gathers into petticoat band, as in making the little "tie around" apron.

(See 21.—Setting Gathers in Band.)

7. Make button-holes in band: one in center front, cutting it *across* the band; and one in each end of band, cutting it *in the direction of the length of the band.*

8. Overhand half-inch lace edging to the hem. A half yard of edging will be needed.

Overhand lace to hem

"And I'm going to shut my eyes and go to sleep while you do it," said Fairy Lady, leaning back in the rocking chair.

She looked so beautiful, Mary Frances would have liked to kiss her— then just to sit still, and look at her; but she thought,

"When she is so dear and kind, and when all the Thimble People want to help me so much, I ought not to loiter."

"I'm here!" said a little tiny voice, and, to be sure, it was Silver Thimble.

"And I!"—it was Needle Book.

"And I!"—Scissors Shears.

"And will you all help?" asked Mary Frances. "I'm so glad!—and then I'll have to do only the new lesson?"

"Only the new,—and here's the Needle-of-Don't-Have-to-Try," said Needle Book.

"Why, everything's nearly done!" exclaimed the little girl in a few minutes. "What wonderful people the Thimble People are!"

"And now," smiled Fairy Lady, "ready for

"I'm here!" said a little tiny voice

PATTERN 13.—DOLL'S DRAWERS

See Insert IV

To cut out—

1. Pin arrow edge of pattern to lengthwise fold of goods, clipping notches carefully.

2. Remove pattern, and cut another leg just like this one.

3. Cut band by pattern of petticoat band.

To make—

1. Make a three-quarter inch hem at the bottom of each piece.

"Here's the 'Needle-of-don't-Have-to-Try.'"

2. Make French seams, or a fell, from bottom of each piece to notch.

3. Make one-eighth inch hem from notch on each side, to top.

4. Gather each piece at top.

5. Pin the end of one narrow hem to double notch (VV) in top of other piece.

6. Pin the center of the then-double material to the center of the band, spreading the fullness of the gathers to the hips and back only—*no fullness in front.*

7. Make button-hole in right hand end of band.

Sew button on other end.

Note.—If trimming is desired,—cut two ruffles, each five inches long, and one and one-half inches wide; and learn to make

Whipped ruffle

37.—Whipped Ruffle

1. Hem the lower edge of ruffles, and overhand lace on the hem.

2. Roll the upper edge of the muslin to the right side of goods, as you have rolled paper edges. Do not fold it. Practice rolling paper if the muslin seems difficult to manage.

3. With a No. 6 needle, and No. 40 cotton, overcast the rolled edge, taking the stitches no deeper than the roll.

4. Draw ruffle up to size needed.

5. Fell the two ends of each ruffle together; and overhand the ruffles to the legs of the drawers, sewing into each "whipping" or overcasting stitch as nearly as possible.

Note.—Fine goods whip more easily than coarse.

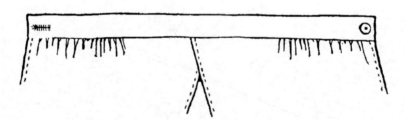

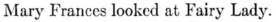

Mary Frances looked at Fairy Lady.

"She's sound asleep," she thought.   "Won't I surprise her!"

.   .   .   .   .   .

"What, all finished?" laughed Fairy Lady.

"Where were you, dear Fairy Lady?" asked Mary Frances.

"I was here—and tapes and tapes away;—away—away—away in Fairy Thimble Land."

She's sound asleep,—won't I surprise her!"

CHAPTER XXV

CAN THE DOLLY TALK

"SAY, are you a really-person? Say, I say, are you real? You look so swell and so beautiful,—can you talk?—say, can you? I wonder if I can touch you, you pretty Mary Marie."

Scissors Shears took a step nearer the doll.

"My, I wish you could talk! I'd like you to hold this muslin for me while I cut out your rompers. What! You won't talk? You just sit looking at me—Stupid! You must think I want something to do! Humph! I wouldn't be a doll, no!

"I wouldn't be a dolly, a dolly, a dolly!
I'd rather be a polly, a polly, a polly!
For a dolly can't talk,
And a polly can talk;
And a dolly can't walk,
And a polly can walk;
I wouldn't be a dolly, a dolly, a dolly!
I'd rather be a polly, a polly, a polly.

"Can you talk?

" 'Pretty Poll!' she can say—'Pretty Doll!'—try it! Say, please try it, Mary Marie! Try it! I say! Doll, try it! If you don't, you'll be sorry! Say 'Pretty Doll!' say it! I say; or,—I'll-cut-your-acquaintance; —then what'll you do?

.   .   .   .   .   .

"You won't get your rompers—maybe;

.   .   .   .   .   .

"You won't get your bloomers—maybe;

.   .   .   .   .   .

"You won't get your pajompers—maybe.

.   .   .   .   .   .

"Oh, you make me tired, you pretty, proud, sweet, lovely-looking thing! Speak, I say, speak! Say 'Bow-wow-wow!' if you can't talk, or even say 'Meow!'

.   .   .   .   .   .

"I'll give it up, I guess.   My, I should think she'd be ashamed not to thank us at all for her fine clothes."

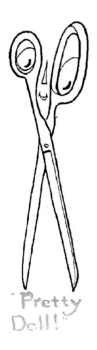

"Pretty Doll!"

"Please try it, Mary Marie"

"Oh, she's only a baby!" said Tommy Pin Cushion. "Babies can't talk!"

"Humph, I s'pose you know, 'cause you're a cry-baby!" exclaimed Scissors Shears.

"I'm not a cry-baby!" exclaimed Tommy Pin Cushion.

"Yo' are! Yo' are!" cried Scissors Shears. "I can prove it!"

"I'm not! Am I, Sewing Bird,—am I?" asked Tommy Pin Cushion, the tears rolling down his fat red cheeks.

"If you could see yourself, you'd know you are!" snapped Scissors Shears.

"Look out there, don't fall!" cried Yard Stick, seeing Scissors Shears toppling dangerously on the table edge.

"Oh, look out yourself," snapped Scissors Shears, "you're just as likely to—"

"I always stand firmly on my three feet," retorted Yard Stick.

"It takes a whole yard to hold them—ha-ha!" laughed Scissors Shears.

Then interrupted Sewing Bird, singing:

"Come, come!
  You're all in fun—
  So why get mad,
  And make all sad?
The little Miss may hear—
So, Tommy, dry up every tear,
And, Thimble, sheath your little spear,
And, Scissors, don't you act so queer,
Or else your Mistress may appear."

'Come, come! You're all in fun—'

Just at that moment in stepped Mary Frances, who had heard every word. The Thimble People looked silly; but she pretended not to notice.

"Oh, my dear Magic and Mystery," she said, "to-day I had another letter from my mother, and she says:

" 'Perhaps you can try to learn a few stitches from the patterns I send you by mail, and you can send me the samplers you make. They will be Sewing Lessons by Mail, and we'll pretend you are taking a Correspondence Course.'

'Oh, Sewing Bird Fairy Lady,—if it doesn't seem a trifle dis-re-spect-a-ble,—I mean dis-re-spect-ful,

'Sewing Lessons by Mail'

—my mother's stitches aren't as nice as mine! Look!"

Mary Frances held up the sampler.

"I want to know what is the right thing to do, Fairy Lady, I would love to surprise my dear mother when I get home; and yet I don't want to deceive her by not telling her that I know something about sewing. What shall I do?"

Fairy Lady smiled thoughtfully. "You might tell her you have a little friend who—"

"Excuse me—friends!" corrected Silver Thimble.

" 'Friends,' " repeated Fairy Lady, "who taught you a little about sewing. It would make your mother happy, I should think."

"Yes!" nodded Mary Frances. "Of course, that's right! And I will feel much nearer to my mother then, and can tell her some day. Do you know, Sewing Bird Fairy Lady—I would,—even as much as I love my dear Grandma,—I would be ex-ceed-ing-ly lonely without my Thimble People."

"Lottie, who lives across the street," she went on, "is lots of fun. I want to teach her to sew some day —may I, Fairy Lady?"

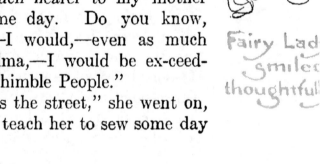

Fairy Lady smiled thoughtfully

'Lottie is lots of fun

"Oh, to be sure," said Fairy Lady, "after you have finished with us."

"But I don't want you to be Never-Nevers!" said Mary Frances.

"Perhaps there'll be a way," suggested Fairy Lady.

"How delightful!" exclaimed Mary Frances. "Oh, I want to show you the pillow cover I bought to-day for Billy."

"How lovely!" exclaimed Scissors Shears, Silver Thimble, Needle Book, Tommy Pin Cushion, and Emery Bag, all at once.

"Yes, isn't it?   Let me read you his letter:"

"For Billy"

> *Woodcraft Camp.*
>
> *Dear Mary Frances:*
>
> *Glad to hear Grandmother is well.   Say, I wish you knew how to sew!   Some of the fellows have the swellest sofa pillows on their cots.   May-be you'll learn some day.   Mother wrote me about the lessons she wants to give you by mail.   It's a rattling good idea.   (I crossed out "rattling" because we're not encouraged to use slang.)*
>
> *See you in September.   So long!*
>
> *Good-bye,   Billy.*

"So you see, Fairy Lady, it is almost absolutely necessary for me to learn to sew."

"On buttons," said Needle Book.

Mary Frances laughed. "Yes, that was a necessity, and I suppose the pillow is a luxury, but I am so pleased that I can make it. See, it has a flag to be worked in red, white, and blue."

"How—?" began Needle Book.

"Why, same as I did the kittens on the doll's apron," said Mary Frances.

"Of course!" smiled the Fairy Lady.

"And you don't need help with it! Isn't that fine! The sooner we finish the lesson,—" began Scissors Shears.

"Hush!" said Fairy Lady, holding up her bodkin wand.

Scissors Shears fell down. "Excuse *me!*" he exclaimed.

"How—?" began Needle Book

"Oh, yes," said Mary Frances. "What is to-day's lesson, please? I'm wasting time!"

"Well," smiled Fairy Lady, "it doesn't matter so much now,—for the King of Thimble Land sent you this package, saying to read the instructions and to ask me any questions you wish at next lesson, if you

"Excuse me!"

do not understand—and he will give you the greatest honor ever bestowed upon a little girl—he will—"

"Lend you—even when not in lessons—the Needle-of-Don't-Have-to-Try," finished Needle Book, bowing before Mary Frances.

"Oh, please bear to His Majesty my gratefulest gratitude!" said Mary Frances, wondering if that were the right way to send a message to a King.

"Oh, my goodness!" screamed Fairy Lady, turning almost white. "There's a cat!" And she immediately changed into the metal sewing bird on the edge of the table.

The metal Sewing Bird

"It's only Jubey!" laughed Mary Frances, "Aunt Maria sent her to me for fear I'd be lonely. I'll never let you come here again, Jubey," she said, picking up the kitten.

Then she opened the package from the King of Thimble Land, and this is what she found:

PATTERN 14.—DOLL'S ROMPERS

See Insert IV

To cut out—

1. Fold goods crosswise. Lay pattern with edge having two rings (oo) on the fold.

2. Pin in place. Cut out.

3. With a large pin, prick through the rows of pinholes marked FRONT. Or use a tracing wheel.

4. Remove pattern.—Spread the rompers open on a table. Cut *one end* of rompers off, along the rows of pinholes.

To cut Neck Band—

Cut a piece of white lawn ten inches long and five inches wide.

5. Fold lawn crosswise.

6. Fold lawn lengthwise. Pin.

7. Place pattern with both the edges having double rings (oo) on *folded* edges of lawn.

Pin in place. Cut out.

To cut Belt—

Cut a piece of lawn fourteen inches long, and four inches wide. Fold *lengthwise,* and *crosswise.*

8. Pin pattern with both edges having double rings (oo) on a fold of lawn. Cut out.

9. Cut sleeve-band with double rings on crosswise fold of lawn.

To make—

1. Turn in both edges of the neck-band one-eighth inch. Baste.

2. Lay rompers flat upon table, and pin and sew neck-band in place in the same way as in Morning Dress.

3. Fold rompers *lengthwise.* From the neck, cut a placket down the fold five inches. *Be certain to cut placket in the back of the rompers.* The back is longer from the neck line than the front.

Fold lengthwise and crosswise

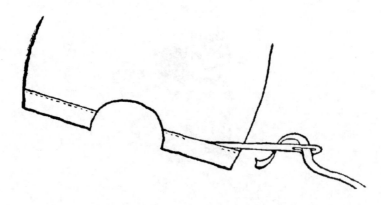

4. Make placket as in Morning Dress.   Fasten with buttons and button-holes.

5. Join rompers under arms with French seam.

6. Join curved edges with French seam.

7. Make a half-inch hem at end of each leg.   *Leave the hem open* one-half inch at the top.   Through this opening run a narrow elastic.   After joining ends of elastic, finish the hemming.

8. If desired, cut a pocket by the pattern of the pinafore-pocket.   (See Insert II.)

Sew in place on left side of rompers in position shown by dotted lines on pattern.

9. To MAKE BELT.—Clip a tiny gash between the two points at each end of belt.   Turn in outer edges of belt one-quarter inch.

Fold belt in half *lengthwise*.   Stitch or overhand the edges. Make button-hole in one end.   Sew button on the other end.

Sew belt in place in middle of back of rompers—as shown on pattern.   Sew to the button-hole side of rompers.

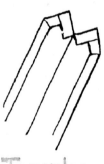

To make Belt

PATTERN 15.—DOLL'S BLOOMERS

See Insert III

1. Cut by pattern of rompers,—*making only as long as the line marked* BLOOMERS.

2. Make in same way as rompers.

3. Make a half-inch hem in the top.   Run elastic in the hem and fasten off in same way as ends of legs of rompers.

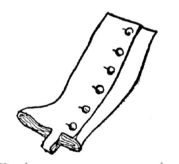

Tack strap under

22. Automobile Bonnet

24. Muff

24. Tippet

28. Polo Cap

INSERT 8

PATTERNS 22·24·28·

2. Automobile Bonnet
1. Muff & Tippet
3. Polo Cap

MUFF
NO. 24
o o

POLO CAP
NO. 28

BONNET
BAND
NO. 22

FRONT

TIPPET
NO. 24

FRONT

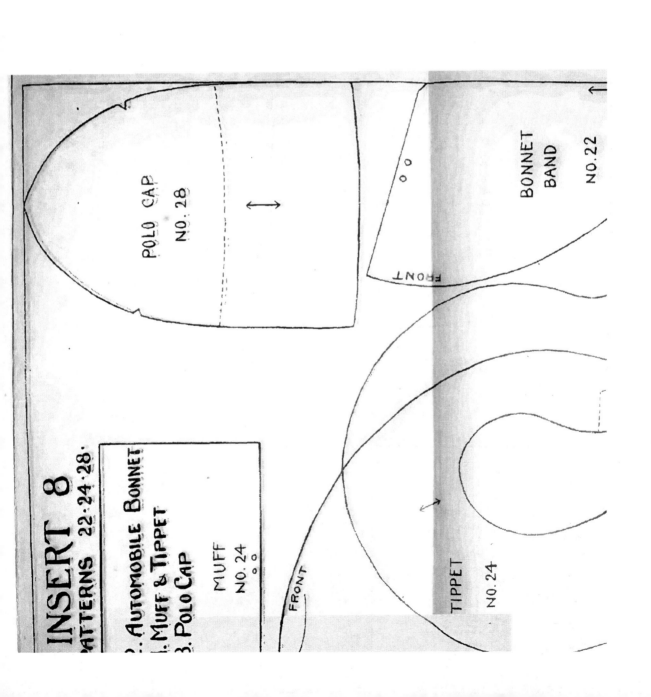

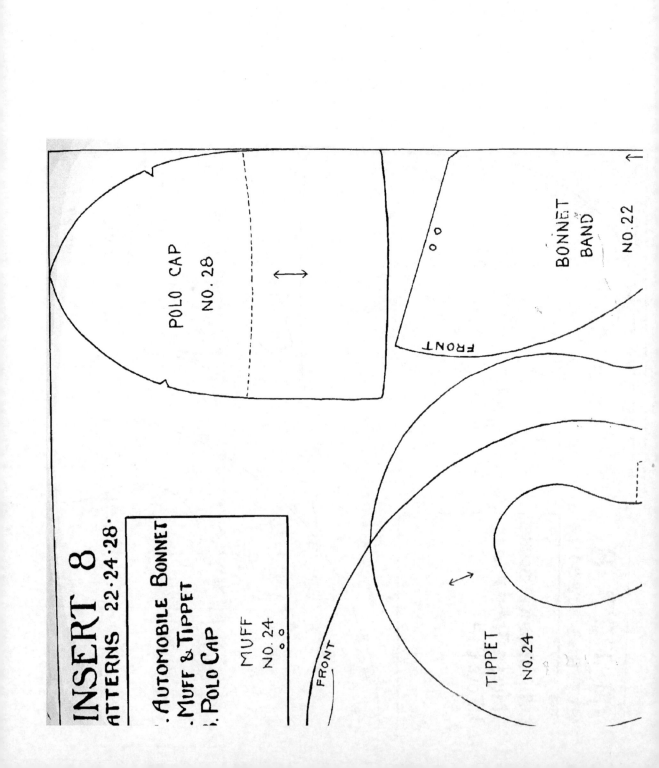

INSERT 8

PATTERNS 22·24·28·

1. AUTOMOBILE BONNET
2. MUFF & TIPPET
3. POLO CAP

MUFF
NO. 24

POLO CAP
NO. 28

BONNET
BAND
NO. 22

FRONT

TIPPET
NO. 24

FRONT

PATTERN 16.—DOLL'S LEGGINGS

See Insert IX

NOTE.—Make leggings of old kid gloves.

1. Cut two of each piece of pattern No. 16.

Pin three pieces *not alike* together.

2. Baste the three pieces not alike, together, matching two single notches, and two double notches, *making top and bottom of legging even.*

3. Stitch in a plain seam.

Sew little "shank" buttons on one side, and cut button-holes in the other side, as indicated on pattern.

Do not attempt to work button-holes in kid.

4. Turn strap under and "tack" (sew with several stitches over and over each other) in place on wrong side of opposite piece, as indicated in pattern.

NOTE.—Always *baste with right sides facing each other,* in making the leggings.

Yours for happy stitches,
His Nibs,
King of Fairy Thimble Land.

The little girl made everything the King sent.

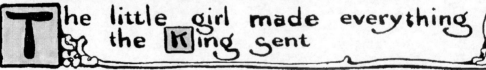

The little girl made everything the King sent

CHAPTER XXVI

A FUR LINED CAPE FOR PARTIES

"Our livings of course"

"I CAN'T wait! I simply cawn't!" Mary Frances paused at the door. It was Scissors Shears again.

"Pray, why 'cawn't' you?" mimicked Tommy Pin Cushion.

'Ah, don't you know? To-day's lesson is so 'el-e-gan-tis-si-mus!' "

"What do we make—I mean what do we help make?" asked Tommy Pin Cushion.

"Our livings, of course," clicked Scissors Shears.

"Oh, you simple, silly old sharp-tongued—!"

"There, there, that will do!" said Scissors Shears; "ask Sewing Bird."

"What do we make, Sewing Bird, please?" asked Tommy Pin Cushion. "I didn't hear."

"A pretty thing
Of funny shape—

A dainty, party
Fur-lined cape,"

sang Sewing Bird.

"Oh, ho! Hee-hee!" laughed Scissors Shears. "I bet we'll have to use Jubey."

"What for?" asked Tommy Pin Cushion.

"For the fur," said Scissors Shears.

"I guess not, I guess not," said Mary Frances stepping into the room. "Use Jubey! I'd rather Mary Marie would never have a fur-lined cape, Magic and Mystery!"

"Of course," said Fairy Lady. "Oh, of course! By the way,—where is that cat?"

"She's down-stairs," said Mary Frances, "hunting mice in the cellar. Grandma asked me to let her be there."

"That's all right," said Fairy Lady, "I feel a little more comfortable to know she is more interested in mice than in birds, at present. You see, she seems to birds very much as lions do to people."

"I'll take good care that she doesn't come up-

"Hunting mice in the cellar

stairs again, dear Fairy Lady," said Mary Frances. "But do I really need fur for to-day's lesson?"

"Have you any fur in Mary Marie's trunk?" asked Fairy Lady.

"No," said Mary Frances. "That is one thing that isn't here."

"What is that?" asked Fairy Lady, peering into the trunk. "Is it very thick white outing flannel?"

"Yes," said Mary Frances, holding up the soft, fleecy material.

"Good!" laughed Fairy Lady. "Good! Now, fetch a bottle of ink and a big toothpick."

"What in the world?" thought the little girl.

"I will show you how to make 'near-ermine' fur," said Fairy Lady, dipping the broad end of the large toothpick into the ink, and making black tail-like marks on the flannelette.

To make 'near-ermine'

"Oh, how sweet!" exclaimed Mary Frances.

"Isn't it pretty?" said Fairy Lady. "This is for the lining. What will the outside of the cape be?"

"Here is some heavy blue silk," said Mary Frances.

"Lovely!" exclaimed Fairy Lady. "You can cut out the cape, then pin it to the flannelette, and cut out

the lining. Then unpin it, and mark the lining like this, to imitate ermine;—and here is another parcel from the Thimble King."

Mary Frances opened the package and read aloud:

PATTERN 17.—DOLL'S FUR-LINED CAPE
See Insert V

To cut out—

1. Pin pattern with the Straight Edge of FRONT on a lengthwise edge of material. Cut out, carefully making all notches.

2. Cut another piece exactly like this.

3. Cut lining in exactly the same way.

4. Cut collar with the two ring (oo) edge of pattern on a lengthwise fold of material.

5. Cut collar lining in same way.

To make—

NOTE.—Make the outside of the cape first. The lining is made in exactly the same way.

1. To MAKE CAPE.—Pin the two pieces together with the right sides facing each other.

2. Baste the long seam (having three single notches). Open the cape.

3. Baste the shoulder seams, matching the notches carefully.

4. Try on doll. Alter cape, if necessary. Stitch seams.

5. Make the lining in the same way.

Mary Frances opened the package

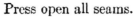

Press open all seams.

6. Turn in outside edges of cape and lining one-quarter inch, except at the neck. Baste. Press.

7. Pin lining in cape, wrong sides facing, carefully fitting seam to seam. Overhand or stitch outside turned-in edges.

8. Baste collar and collar-lining together. Stitch an eighth-of-an-inch seam along all edges except the neck-edge.

Turn inside-out. Baste along edges. Press.

9. Sew the collar to the cape, in same way as an apron band, first pinning the double notches in the outside of the collar to the double notches in the outside of the cape.

10. Fasten cape with a hook and eye.

"My, I do hope such finery won't make Mary Marie vain!" said Fairy Lady.

"No," said Mary Frances, "I think it won't. I've explained to her that she must divide with all her sisters-in-law, and step-sisters, her whole outfit. It seems almost like a trousseau."

"That's true and sew!" exclaimed Scissors Shears.

"My, I do hope such finery won't make Mary Marie vain"

CHAPTER XXVII

A "DRESS-UP" DRESS

"GOOD-AFTERNOON, your Seamstress-ship," welcomed Sewing Bird.

"Good-afternoon, dear Thimble People," said Mary Frances. "I was so sorry that I had to miss last week's lesson! Grandma didn't take her afternoon out, and little Lottie was over here to play."

"I know," said Scissors Shears. "I heard you; I had on my long ears."

"You did!" laughed Mary Frances. "Well, did you hear me promise to give her some little helps in dressing her doll? I would dearly love to make something for her doll—a dress, I think. She is just the size of Mary Marie."

"What's her name?" asked Scissors Shears.

"The doll's name, do you mean? Katy-did."

"Good-
afternoon

"Oh, bless my bill!
Oh, what a name!

[217]

> If Katy-did—
> It is a shame,"

sang Sewing Bird.

"Katy did what?" asked Scissors Shears, staring at Mary Frances.

"Katy-did Nice," answered Mary Frances.

"You mean nicely, I think," said Scissors Shears.

"No," said Mary Frances. "Nice is Lottie's last name. The whole name of Lottie's doll is—Katy-did Nice. Can't I make her a dress?"

"Well," answered Sewing Bird, slowly, "if you do, you may be asked about us; and if you answer the question truly, we'll never, never be able to do anything more."

"Never! Never!" exclaimed Mary Frances. "I'd rather never make the dress for Katy-did Nice."

> "If you wait
> And do not fret,
> You'll get your wishes
> Even yet,"

"Katie-did
what?"

sang Sewing Bird.

"Katie-did Nice."

"Oh, thank you, dear Magic and Mystery," said the little girl. "I will be patient,—indeed I will!"

"Well, then," said Fairy Lady, "here is to-day's message, and gift from the King of Thimble Land."

Mary Frances took the package. It was tied with golden thread and fastened with a sunbeam.

"Press the sunbeam," smiled Fairy Lady, "and the package will open."

Out fell

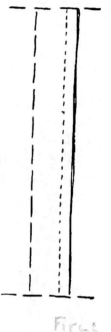

First tuck

PATTERN 18.—DOLL'S AFTERNOON DRESS
See Insert VI

To Tuck Dress—

1. Cut the material twenty-four inches long, and eighteen inches wide.

2. Find center by folding the goods crosswise. Crease.

3. Spread material open. Measure five and one-half inches down on both sides of the crease.

Mark across the goods with pins—then with red bastings.

4. Fold material lengthwise. Crease well, between red bastings.

Spread the material open. Run a blue basting thread down this center crease.

5. Measure three-quarter inch from the blue basting to the right, *along the red bastings*. Mark with pins.

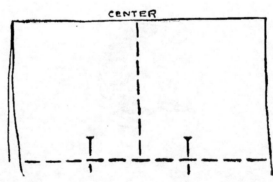

Mark tucks each side center basting

6. Fold and crease from pin to pin, being careful to keep a straight line.

7. Baste three-eighth of an inch from edge of fold, through the double cloth.

8. Do same to left of center crease.

9. To make another tuck—Lay tuck already made, backward toward center

Then measure from edge of fold of tuck one and one-half inches, along each red basting line.   Mark with pins.

10. Make new tuck in same way as first tuck.

There should be two tucks each side of center crease.

11. Stitch tucks along the basting lines.

NOTE.—When tucking is finished, compare it with the pin-holes on pattern.

ALL THESE TUCKS are laid and creased to the bottom of goods before cutting out dress.

To Cut Out Dress—

1. Fold goods crosswise.   Pin pattern in place, with edge having double rings on the fold.   Cut out.

2. With a pin, prick through the dotted belt lines.

3. Cut four collar pieces.   Pin arrow (➤➤─➤) edge of collar pattern on a lengthwise edge of goods.

4. Cut two belts, with double rings on a lengthwise fold of material.

5. Cut two sleeve-bands by sleeve-band pattern of Morning Dress (Pattern 9).

6. To Cut Skirt Trimming Band.—Remove pattern from

Cut
four
collar
pieces

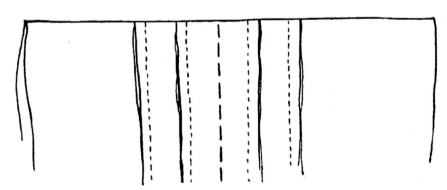

Two tucks each side center

dress.   Spread open the skirt part.   Lay it upon the plain trimming material.   Pin in place.

7. Cut off at edge of skirt.   Make this band one and one-half inches wide.   Cut two such bands.

To Make Dress—

1. Join seams of skirt trimming-band.
2. Stitch sleeve-bands in place, as for Morning Dress.
3. Make placket and make button-holes, and sew on buttons.
4. Join underarm with French seams.
5. Face (right side of) bottom of dress with skirt trimming-band in the following way:

"Facing" is making a false hem.

On the wrong side of the skirt, lay the skirt trimming-band with the lower edge even with the bottom of the skirt.

Baste.   Stitch one-quarter inch from edge.

6. Remove bastings.   Turn band over to right side.

Crease along the seam.   Baste along the seam.

Turn in edge of trimming-band (or facing) one-quarter inch.

Baste band flat against dress.   Stitch (or hem) in place.

7. Make each belt in same way as belt for rompers.
8. Make two collars in same way as collar for fur-lined cape. Pattern 17.
9. Sew collars fast to dress, first pinning notch to the fold-crease of the shoulder at the neck.

Attach collars to dress in same way as underwaist to flannel petticoat.

10. Pin belts in place shown on pattern.   Fasten each belt

Sew belt
fast
through
a button

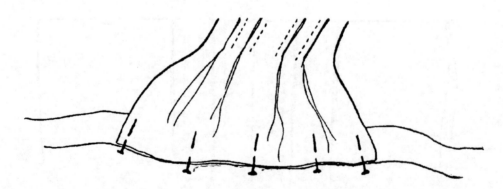

Lay edge of skirt on trimming band

in two places only.   On the point, which lies over a plait, sew belt fast, through a button.

These belts hold the fullness of the dress, under arms, in place.

Best wishes to the little girl who "tries."

King Thimble.

"How beautiful!" exclaimed Mary Frances. "Please thank His Majesty, dear Thimble People."

"Can you get along without our help, please?" asked Scissors Shears.

"Well," said Mary Frances, "the Needle-of-Don't-Have-to-Try, you know,—"

"But," said Scissors Shears, hopping up and down, "what I want to know is,—can you cut all that without help?   May I ask what goods you will use for the afternoon dress?"

"This pretty red-dotted lawn," said Mary Frances, "and this fine white lawn for the guimpe!"

"Will you, may I ask, please,—will you leave the lawn and pattern on the sewing table?"

"Oh, I know!" cried Mary Frances.   "You want to help by cutting them out, Scissors Shears—but I will do my own *making*,— thank you."

Can you
get along
without
our help?"

"How beautiful!"

When the afternoon dress was finished, Mary Frances slipped it on Mary Marie, sat her in her rocking chair, then stepped outside, and peeped in to see what the Thimble People would do.   In a minute, they gathered in a circle around the pretty doll, and began singing:

> "Proudie!   Proudie!
> Aren't you a little Proudie!
> Proudie! Proudie!
> Aren't you a little Proudie!"

Mary Marie looked pleased, but couldn't say a word.

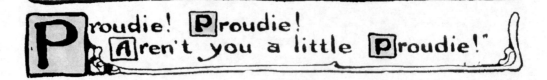

"Proudie! Proudie! Aren't you a little Proudie!"

CHAPTER XXVIII

MARY MARIE HAS A PARTY DRESS

"DEARIE me! Thimble People," exclaimed Mary Frances. "I'm so excited! I'm so excited! Mary Marie has been invited to a party."

"To a party!" exclaimed Scissors Shears. "To a party,—excuse me, but don't you mean, 'by a party?'"

"How could you buy a party?" asked Tommy Pin Cushion.

"It's been known to be done," answered Scissors Shears.

"Will her mother let her go?" asked Silver Thimble anxiously.

"Yes, indeed," laughed Mary Frances. "If she has a party dress—"

"What a guess!
Why, what a guess!
Next lesson is
A party dress!"

[224]

sang Sewing Bird, hopping on one leg on the table, and fluttering her wings,

> "Mary Marie,
>   How sweet she'll be
>   In finery:
>   Not spoiled she'll be
>   By vanity,
>   Or finery."

"Just be her own sweet self, won't you, dear?" said Mary Frances, hugging the dolly close.

> "If you were
>   As pretty as she,
> You might be
>   Spoiled by finery,"

Fluttering her wings

sang Tommy Pin Cushion, pointing to Scissors Shears. "By the way, how's business?"

"Dull! Fatty," began Scissors Shears, "You—" then, seeing Mary Frances' look, he added lamely, "Pretty is as pretty does, and beauty is only skin-deep.

"Just be her own sweet self"

If you lost your skin, Tommy, we'd knock all the stuf-
fin's out o' you!''

"Hush!" whispered Sewing Bird,

> "Now, let's to work,
>   Now, let's not shirk,
>   But sew with purpose hearty!
>   With love and fun,
>   Work is begun
>   On the dress for dolly's party!"

"Oh, thank you," exclaimed Mary Frances, opening Mary Marie's trunk. "What shall we use, Magic
and Mystery?"

"Let me see?" said Fairy Lady, flying down beside
the trunk.

Mary Frances was too surprised to say anything
when she saw the lovely gauzy wings spread out, and
Fairy Lady sailing down from the table.

"Oh," said the little fairy in her bird-like voice,
"little Lady Seamstress, this is only a small surprise
compared to the lovely ones in store for you."

"More yet, dear Fairy Lady?" asked Mary Frances,
her eyes opening in wonder. "Why, it seems to me—"

"Hush!"
whispered
Sewing
Bird

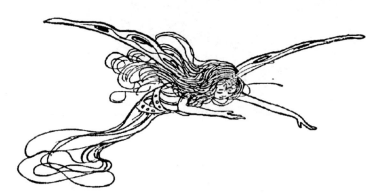

Fairy Lady sailing down from the table

Let me see. said Fairy Lady

"I must not tell you another word," said the little lady; "I shouldn't have said even that!"

"Oh, I wouldn't have dared whisper that," said Tommy Pin Cushion to Emery Bag. "Why, the King would have shaken the stuffing out of me!"

"This," exclaimed Fairy Lady, "is just the thing to make a party dress for Mary Marie," and she held up a piece of most beautiful fabric.

"What is it?" asked Mary Frances. "I didn't see that in the trunk!"

"Didn't you?" asked Fairy Lady.

Mary Frances held up the sparkling goods. It was very, very fine, and thin, yet not veil-like. It shone like spun glass, and was made of the colors of the rainbow.

"How exquisite!" breathed the little girl. "Isn't it beautiful! Please, dear Fairy Lady, where did it come from?"

"It came," said Fairy Lady, "from your friend, the King of Fairy Thimble Land."

"Oh," said Mary Frances. "Did you, dear Fairy Lady, did you bring it?"

"What is it?"

I wouldn't have dared whisper that!

"In this," nodded Fairy Lady, and she held up a little satchel that looked like Mary Frances' mother's pearl earring.

"Will it go in such a tiny satchel?" asked the little girl, in an awed voice.

"Yes," smiled Fairy Lady, "but the pattern takes up more room."

"Did you carry that, too?" asked Mary Frances.

"Yes, in a little suit case," said Fairy Lady.

"May I see the pattern?" asked Mary Frances.

She wondered how Fairy Lady would get back on the table, but the little lady spread her wings again—this time showing the lovely coloring and golden tips.

Flying high above the table, she came down and settled herself in the doll's rocking chair.

Then she spread open

She held up a little satchel

PATTERN 19.—DOLL'S GUIMPE (FOR PARTY DRESS)

See Insert III

Suggestions for material.—Dimity or lace.

To cut out—

1. Pin pattern with edge having two rings (oo) on a *crosswise* fold of goods. Cut out.

"Yes, in a little suit case"

2. Cut guimpe sleeve-band, with arrow lengthwise of material.
To make—

1. Gather end of each sleeve.

2. Fold sleeve-band through center, lengthwise. (See dotted line on pattern.)

3. Sew sleeve-bands in place at ends of sleeves, in same way as band of little "tie around apron."

4. Join guimpe under arms with French seams.

5. Make a half-inch hem down each side of back.

6. Make a half-inch hem in bottom of guimpe. Through this hem run a narrow tape, threaded into a bodkin.

7. Turn the *narrowest hem possible* in the neck. Do not attempt to hem this with hemming stitches, but overhand it closely.

8. Overhand narrow lace edging in the neck and sleeves.

9. Make three button-holes, and sew on buttons.

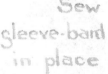

Sew sleeve-band in place

PATTERN 20.—DOLL'S PARTY DRESS
See Insert X

Suggestions for material.—Flowered dimity or lawn.
To cut out—

1. The skirt should be cut: five and one-half inches long—with the *lengthwise* of the material.

Thirty-two inches wide—*across* the material.

2. To Cut Out the Waist—

Fold material crosswise. Pin pattern with edge having two rings (oo) on the fold. Cut out. Remove pattern.

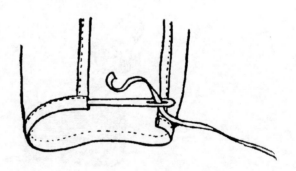

Through hem run a narrow tape

3. To Cut Neck.—Cut pattern along the row of pinholes, marked FRONT.

Fold back along other row of pinholes.

Spread waist *open* on table.

Pin pattern in place on one end of waist. Cut neck by the turned-in V-shaped outline.

To make—

1. Join skirt and make placket as in white lawn petticoat.

2. Make a three-quarter inch hem at the bottom.

Gather top, using two gathering threads. Begin each thread in center top of skirt.

3. Fold waist *lengthwise.* Cut open the back *from center of square* of neck. Make half-inch hems down the backs.

4. Make a *narrow* hem around the neck-opening.

5. Spread waist open on table. Cut a piece of baby ribbon two and one-quarter inches long. Cut another piece one and one-half inches long.

6. Fasten, by sewing through a bead, one end of each piece of ribbon to one side of the V-shaped neck opening, in the place shown by the pinholes in the pattern.

7. Fasten other end in same way, making the front neck opening one and one-quarter inches wide at the top, and three-quarters of an inch wide at the pointed end.

8. Join with French seam *from notches* to *bottom* of waist.

9. Hem armholes above the seams.

Gather across the shoulder fold, making the gathered goods measure *one inch across.* Fasten thread.

Gather across the shoulder

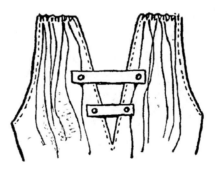

Fasten ribbon by sewing through a bead

10. Cut a belt of half-inch-wide white tape, making it eleven inches long.

Gather bottom of waist.   Turn in ends of tape belt one-quarter inch.

11. Baste gathers of waist flat to tape belt, having tape on wrong side.   Baste gathers of skirt flat to other edge of tape belt.

Stitch in place.   Sew lace insertion, or ribbon beading over the gathers on the right side.

12. Make button-holes, and sew on buttons.

13. Trim the hems around the neck-opening and armholes with

38.—FRENCH KNOTS

1. Thread embroidery needle with embroidery cotton.   Make knot.   Draw needle through from wrong side.

2. With left hand, wrap cotton, *where it comes through the material,* three times around the needle, holding needle with right hand.

3. Holding the coiled thread firmly in place with left thumb, insert needle-point downward, at place where it first came through.   Pull through to wrong side.

4. Push needle upward where next stitch is to be made. Pull through to right side.   Proceed as above.

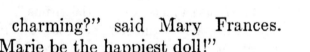

French Knots

"Won't it be charming?" said Mary Frances. "Oh, won't Mary Marie be the happiest doll!"

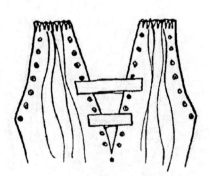

Trim with french knots

"But how can you keep it a secret, if she goes to a party?" asked Scissors Shears anxiously. "I don't want to be a Never-Never."

"Oh," said Mary Frances, "the party isn't to be given until next summer. She's only invited—that's all."

"Strike me pink!" exclaimed Tommy Pin Cushion. "I was feeling scared white."

"Strike me pink!"

"Shows how silly it is to worry," said Emery Bag.

"I beg all your pardons," said Mary Frances. "I didn't mean to be—to take advantage. I almost forgot how long it is till next summer. I am very sorry if I did wrong."

"Gives you longer to finish the dress," said Fairy Lady. "There's a good deal of work on it."

"I'll work very hard," said Mary Frances, "and I'll be more careful what I say in the future."

"We understand, of course we do,
That your kind heart is always true;
You wouldn't do a thing that you
Would not have others do to you,"

Sand Sewing Bird

sang Sewing Bird,—and perhaps, the little bird smiled.

.   .   .   .

This is how the dress looked when Mary Frances had finished it.

"Mary Marie is going to a party"

CHAPTER XXIX

MARY MARIE GOES AUTOMOBILING

"OH, my feathers and oh, my eye!" Sewing Bird was screaming, as Mary Frances came to the sewing room door for the next lesson.

"Why, what's the matter, Sewing Bird?" asked Mary Frances.

"Not for myself, but quite contrary—
'Twas for the sake of Dick Canary!"

sang Sewing Bird frantically.

"Why, what is the matter, dear little bird?" again asked Mary Frances.

Sewing Bird replied:

"While I was sitting here in state,
Just what happened I'll now relate:

"A gentle scratching at the door,
A gentle foot-step on the floor,

[234]

Then Jubey, black as a blackberry,
Looked up at pretty Dick Canary,
And what he said, to me seemed clear:—
'Ah, bird, your voice is very dear!
Your feathers shine like purest gold
As in the sun they do unfold;
Oh, sing to me, you lovely thing,
Oh, sing and sing and sing and sing!'

"Then Dick Canary hurt his throat,
He sang so loud on every note.

"'Now, people love to eat of chicken—
If I stole one, I'd get a lickin',
And then you'd hear an awful scream—
"Why don't you give that cat ice-cream?"
A chicken and a bird to me
Seem much alike—do they to thee?
How classic is your pretty voice,
I love to hear you make that noise.
Oh, sing to me, you lovely thing,
Oh, sing and sing and sing and sing.'

"Dick
Canary
hurt his
throat"

"Ah, bird, your voice is very dear!"

"Then Dick Canary hurt his throat,
He sang so loud on every note.

" 'Music has charm to soothe, I believe,
The wild instincts that in me breathe.
How horrible your lonely fate,
To be behind that golden gate.
If I for you undo the bars,
Perhaps you'll soar beyond the stars.
Where go birds-souls—I really wonder—
It makes me sit and sit and ponder.
Oh, sing to me, you lovely thing,
Oh, sing and sing and sing and sing.'

"Then Dick Canary hurt his throat
He sang so loud on every note.

"He sang
so loud
on every
note"

" 'If I undo the bars for thee,
And from the cage thy sweet life free—
Well, folks love chicken, this I know—
Are you a chicken?   Yes! I trow!'

.   .   .   .   .   .

"Just then, I heard you on the stair,
Dear Miss, and cried out, then and there;

"I heard you on the stair"

Not for myself—but quite contrary—
'Twas for the sake of Dick Canary.''

"I met Jubey scudding into the kitchen," laughed Mary Frances, "frightened to death,—she looked. I can't understand how she got up-stairs, Magic and Mystery. I said to her: 'Jubey, you'll get no sympathy from me if you've been up-stairs.' "

"The strange part is," said Fairy Lady, "that Dick Canary seemed to like it."

"'Flattery sounds
    Sweet to the ear,
Even from those
    We ought to fear,'

my Grandma says," replied Mary Frances.

"Oh, yes," said Fairy Lady. "I do believe that is so; now, for to-day's plans."

"This time," said Mary Frances, rather shame-facedly, "it is a real event. Mary Marie has been invited to take an automobile ride with Lottie's ten children."

"Dick Canary seemed to like it"

"This time it is a real event"

"Oh, how delightful!" exclaimed Fairy Lady, "and so opportune!"

"Opportune," thought Mary Frances. "Opportune—that must mean 'just right.'"

"Yes," nodded Fairy Lady, as though reading her thoughts, "it is 'just right'—for I have to-day the

PATTERN 21.—DOLL'S AUTOMOBILE COAT
See Insert VII

To cut out—

1. Fold goods crosswise. Pin pattern with edge having two rings (oo) on fold. Cut out.

2. Remove pattern. Spread coat open on a table.

3. Cut pattern along the *one* row of pinholes marked FRONT. (See Directions on Insert VII.) Fold pattern backward along the other row of pinholes.

4. Pin pattern in place on *one* end of coat.

5. Cut neck along the V-shaped lines.
Remove pattern.

6. Cut goods open from point of V-shaped neck, to bottom of coat.
This makes the front-opening.

7. Cut two collars with edge of pattern having the two rings (oo) on lengthwise fold of material.

8. Cut two cuffs with edge of pattern having two rings (oo) on lengthwise fold of material.

So opportune!

That must mean "just right"

To make—

1. To face the front-openings:—

Spread coat open upon a piece of the material of which it is made, right sides facing.

2. Baste along front-opening, and *around* the neck, through the material underneath.

Cut open the underneath-material, along the opening of the coat.

3. Cut underneath-material off, one and one-half inches from edge of front-opening and *around* the neck.

4. Stitch facing in place one-quarter inch from edges. Remove bastings. Turn facings over to wrong side. Baste edge, along enclosed seam.

5. Closely notch, or "pink" the "raw" edges of facings.

Baste facings down along notched edges. Press.

Stitch (or "tack") facings down near the notched edges.

6. Baste facings on ends of sleeves, on wrong side of coat.

Stitch one-quarter inch from edge. Remove bastings.

7. Turn facings over to right side, and baste along the turned edges. Turn down one-quarter inch at top, and stitch down.

8. Join coat under arms with French seams.

9. Make collar as for Fur-lined Cape.

10. Matching notches carefully, baste collar on coat, and sew in place as in making Fur-lined Cape.

11. Make a three-quarter inch hem at bottom of coat.

12. Fasten coat with two large buttons and button-holes.

To fasten coat

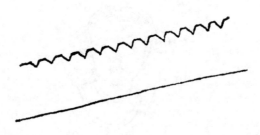

Closely notch edges of facings

PATTERN 22.—DOLL'S AUTOMOBILE BONNET

See Insert VIII

To cut—

1. Fold goods lengthwise.

Pin pattern with edge having two rings (oo) on the fold. Clip the notch carefully.

2. In cutting Bonnet Band and lining:—Pin pattern with edge having two rings (oo) on a lengthwise fold of material.

To make—

1. One-quarter inch from edge, gather circular part of bonnet from notch in center back to notch in center front. Gather other side of circle.

2. Baste lining to Bonnet Band.

Stitch one-quarter inch from front edge.

3. Remove bastings. Open the band. Join ends in a plain seam. Fold lining down inside band, and baste along the circular seam. Stitch one-quarter inch from edge.

4. To Join Band to Bonnet:—Proceed just as in attaching collar to Fur-Lined Cape.

First pin single center-front notch of bonnet and of band together.

Then the double notches.

Then single center-back notch of bonnet to *seam* of band.

Baste and sew in place, hemming down the lining.

Attach ribbon-strings at the double notches.

Attach ribbon strings

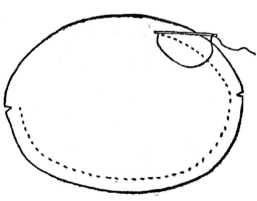

Gather from notch to notch

NOTE.—Trim bonnet with bunch of ribbon-rosette flowers, sewed on left side.

Fold back the bonnet band through the middle. (See dotted line on pattern.)

"My dear Thimble People!" exclaimed Mary Frances, after working a long while with the Needle-of-Don't-Have-to-Try. "Never did a child have such lovely friends—never! Look at this dear little coat!"

"We love all children who are patient, and try to do their best!" smiled Fairy Lady. "So many are forgetful, or impolite and impatient."

"I'm afraid I'm sometimes all of those," said Mary Frances.

"This dear little coat"

"But in your very down-deep heart,
  You never think the things that smart;
  Your heart is really always kind—
  Sometimes you're wrong, and sometimes blind,—
  But those who know you well, know this:
  To make all right, you give a kiss—
  Not just an ordinary kiss—
  It says, 'Please just forgive me this!' "

Trim bonnet with ribbon-rosette flowers

"And that is why you are loved so much!" Sewing Bird sang.

Mary Frances took Mary Marie, all dressed in her new automobile clothes, out to the automobile which had just pulled up in front of the door. And Scissors Shears, and Tommy Pin Cushion, and Emery Bag, and Pen Cil, and Needle Book, and all the other Thimble People, waved their cunning little hands.

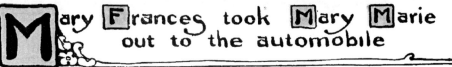

Mary Frances took Mary Marie out to the automobile

CHAPTER XXX

MARY MARIE GOES IN BATHING

MARY FRANCES tip-toed into the sewing room.

"S'sh! s'sh!" she said. Oh, Thimble People, I've,—oh, dear me! Oh, Magic and Mystery,—I've got the bath-tub half full of water. It's the ocean, I have my sail-boat on it, and Mary Marie is going in bathing—when I've finished my lesson. I just dipped her feet in to see how she'd like it—I can't exactly say Grandma would approve—but Mother would let me, I think.

"Isn't it strange? My grandmother — my mother's mother—doesn't think exactly as *her* little girl, my mother, does. Now, I generally always think almost exactly what my mother thinks is right."

"'Generally always almost exactly,'" whispered Scissors Shears to Tommy Pin Cushion. "That's the way I agree with Sewing Bird."

"And you, Tommy Pin Cushion?" asked Emery Bag.

[243]

"And you, Tommy Pin Cushion?"

"And I—" began Tommy Pin Cushion.

"Hush up!" said Scissors Shears. "You're always stuck in! You keep quiet, nobody gets a chance to talk for you!"

Tommy Pin Cushion got very red in the face.

"It—seems—to—me,—" he stammered.

"Yes, there you go again!" exclaimed Scissors Shears. "Just as I said! Always forever trying to stick your bill in—though I must say—you haven't much of a bill—I must say that!"

"Stop quarreling!" exclaimed Mary Frances.

"If Mary Marie goes in bathing," said Fairy Lady, "here is just the thing she'll need:

PATTERN 23.—DOLL'S BATHING SUIT

1. The Bathing Suit is made by the pattern of Rompers (see Insert IV) and of

2. Doll's Lawn Petticoat.   (See Pattern 12.)

Cut skirt only five inches long, and do not make a tuck.

Suggestions for Material—

Red or blue flannel, trimmed with white braid.

NOTE.—The skirt may be gathered or plaited.

Make the opening of the rompers in front. Face the front openings with a strip of lining material one-half inch wide.

Doll's Bathing Suit

Tommy Pin Cushion got red in the face

16. Leggings

25. Sun Bonnet

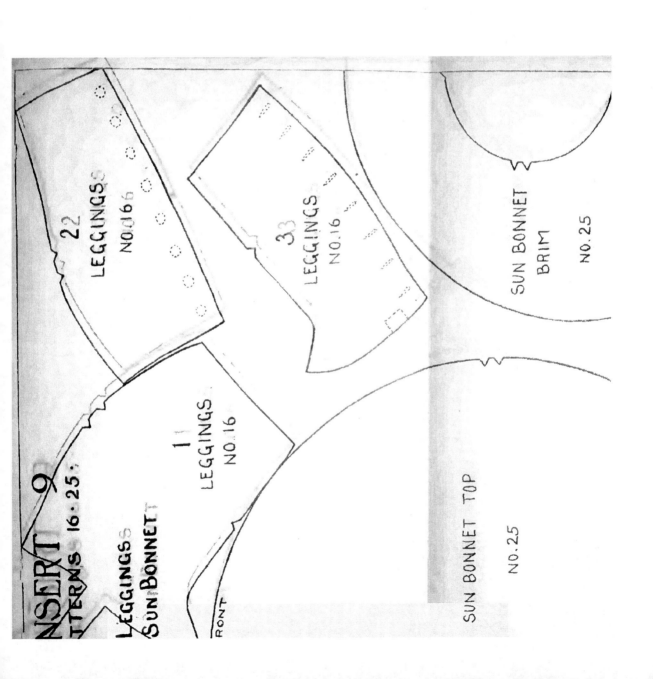

INSERT 9
PATTERNS 16 · 25 ·

LEGGINGS
SUN BONNET

FRONT

22
LEGGINGS
NO.16 b

33
LEGGINGS
NO.16

11
LEGGINGS
NO.16

SUN BONNET
BRIM

NO.25

SUN BONNET TOP

NO.25

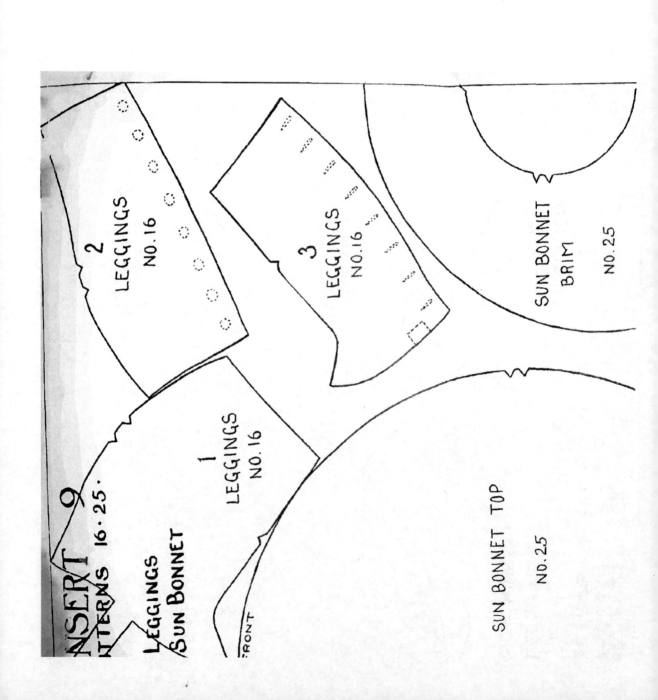

INSERT 9

PATTERNS 16·25·

LEGGINGS
SUN BONNET

2
LEGGINGS
NO.16

3
LEGGINGS
NO.16

1
LEGGINGS
NO.16

FRONT

SUN BONNET
BRIM

NO.25

SUN BONNET TOP

NO.25

Make eyelets in the facings, and lace Bathing Suit together through the eyelets.

"This is splendid!" exclaimed Mary Frances, as she began to cut out the suit. "Grandma is to be away several hours to-day. I would miss her terribly if it were not for you, dear friends. We have such fun—she and I—almost as much as Father and I, or Mother and I, or Bill and I—or, just as much as Lottie and I! But I want to get these lovely things made for my dear Mary Marie before Grandma comes back."

"Then," smiled Fairy Lady, "you must learn to make:

39.—EYELETS

For practice, use a folded and basted piece of muslin, as for button-holes.

1. Pierce the cloth with a "stiletto," or very large needle-punch, breaking as few threads as possible.

2. Work the edges of the hole with over-and-over overhanding stitches, close together as possible. Hold work over forefinger of left hand.

NOTE.—In making a large eye-hole, mark a circle with running stitch, cut out close inside the thread. Turn back the edges and work closely with button-hole stitch.

"Oh," exclaimed Mary Frances.   "Now, when I finish this, my Mary Marie can splash and splash— but I'll not get them done to-day,—even with the Needle-of-Don't-Have-to-Try!"

"But you will finish them quite soon," said Fairy Lady, "I feel certain."

"You do believe in me, dear little Lady," said Mary Frances.

> "Faith in us
>   Makes us do, and be,
> Far better than
>   We think or see,"

sang Sewing Bird.

"If she doesn't get them done soon, Mary Marie will lose her bath," whispered Tommy Pin Cushion, giggling, and he began to recite,—

> "Oh, Missy, may I go in to swim?
>   Oh, yes, my darling rub-dub;
> Hang your clothes on a towel-rack limb,
>   But don't go near the bath-tub."

whispered Tommy Pin Cushion

"Tommy Pin Cushion!" exclaimed Mary Frances, picking him up and putting him on the window sill.

"Excuse me!" spoke up the little fellow, looking out of the window, "but here comes your grandmother."

"I better run and let the water out of the bath-tub," said Mary Frances.

.   .   .   .

"Mary Marie didn't get her bath!" exclaimed Scissors Shears. "She didn't get her bath!"

"Well, she went in bathing, anyhow," said Tommy Pin Cushion. "Didn't you see? Both her feet were wet!"

"That's how wet you'd get if you went swimming," said Scissors Shears. "She'll go in bathing when the little Miss finishes her suit—maybe."

Mary Marie is going in bathing!

CHAPTER XXXI

Muffs and Caps and Prettiest Traps

"THIS letter says," explained Mary Frances, "this letter says, oh, Thimble Friends, that my mother and father are coming home in two weeks,—and Billy, too. I must hurry to finish my lessons. Oh, dear, dear! Why, what's the matter, Scissors Shears—and Tommy Pin Cushion—and Emery Bag?"

'It means 'au revoir' but not good-bye'

"It means good-bye!" sobbed Scissors Shears.

"It means good-bye!" sobbed Tommy Pin Cushion.

"It means good-bye!" whimpered Emery Bag.

"It means 'au revoir,' but not good-bye," sang Sewing Bird.

"Oh, it do, do it?" said Scissors Shears, looking sharply at Sewing Bird.

"Does it, Magic and Mystery?" asked Mary Frances.

"It doesn't mean good-bye," answered Fairy Lady. "But I can't explain it until some time later."

"My, I'm relieved!" said Mary Frances. "So—what is to-day's lesson, dear Fairy Lady?"

> "For Mary Marie more lovely things
> The Fairy Lady to you brings,—
> A little muff, and tippet of fur,
> A sweet little summer cap for her,
> A dainty little cross-stitch bag—
> But I must stop for fear I'll brag,"

sang Fairy Lady. Then stooping, she drew these patterns from under the rocking chair cushion:

A Muff and Tippet

PATTERN 24.—DOLL'S MUFF AND TIPPET
See Insert VIII

Directions for making Doll's Fur Muff and Tippet.

1. Cut tippet from heavy flannelette—arrow on lengthwise of goods.

2. Mark with ink to imitate Ermine. Turn in edge one-quarter of an inch. Baste.

3. Cut lining of silk.

4. From sheet-cotton cut a lining one-half of an inch smaller than pattern edges.

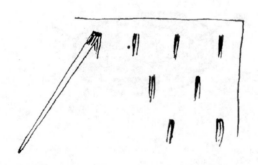

5. Baste lining to this.   Turn edges of lining over this, and baste.

Sew on hook and eye, at the neck.

6. Baste linings to outside, and "slip stitch" together.

40.—SLIP STITCH

Is like hemming stitch, but the needle is slipped along about one-half of an inch—for each stitch.   The needle is put into the material directly below where your thread is last brought out.

7. Cut and make muff in same way as tippet.   Then, join the ends of the outside in a plain seam.   Open the seam, and hem down the lining seam.   Turn muff to right side.

Run through the muff a white cord.

PATTERN 25.—DOLL'S SUN BONNET
See Insert IX

Cut out and make in same way as Automobile Bonnet.

Suggestions for material—Figured organdy, with lawn brim; or, brim of white pique.

If pique is used for brim do not make brim double, but blanket-stitch the outer edge, and bind the seam where attached to bonnet.

To Bind a Seam

To Bind a Seam.—Cut a narrow bias strip of goods.   Baste it even with the seam on the wrong side.   Stitch in place.   Turn it over the seam.   Turn in the raw edge.   Baste.   Hem down. This may be done with tape, which will not need edges turned in.

Pattern 26.—Doll's Work Bag

Use checked silk-gingham.

Cut same as Doll's Laundry Bag.   (Pattern I.)

On the ends of the bag, work in cross-stitch, the "bunny" design given on this page.

Make bag in same way as Doll's Laundry Bag.

> "In the morning, before 'twas light,
> Two little bunnies began to fight;
> They fit all day and they fit all night:
> That made each such a mad little bun?
> Because both were in cross-stitch done,"

sang Scissors Shears.

"I'll excuse you for interrupting," said Fairy Lady, "but when Mary Marie gets all these things,

> "Oh! won't she be grand!
> Won't she be grand!
> There's not a lady
> In the land
> Who can with her compare."

"I'll excuse you for interrupting

Bunny design

Then Scissors Shears interrupted again,

"Alas! Alack!
If on my back
I wore such lovely, lovely clothes
I'd never freeze my little toes,
Nor wiggle up my little nose."

"Oh," laughed Tommy Pin Cushion,

"If I could wear such lovely garb,
I then would feel no deadly barb
Of arrows aiméd at my heart.
That's a grand rhyme! Am I that smart?"

Then Sewing Bird,

"Enough of this fun
For to-day.
Away, you rascals—
Run away!

"but,

"Mary Frances, if you please,
  Take the patterns, and make these
  Pretty things—a lot of fun!
  Let me see them when they're done."

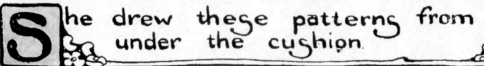

She drew these patterns from under the cushion.

CHAPTER XXXII

WHO STOLE MARY MARIE'S CLOTHES

MARY FRANCES stepped into the sewing room. She had Mary Marie's trunk under her arm.

"Oh, did you finish the cute little muff and tippet, and work bag, your Seamstress-ship?" asked Fairy Lady.

"Yes, indeed,—I'll show them to you," said Mary Frances, lifting the lid of the trunk.

"Oh, mercy!" she cried, "Oh, dear! Oh, my! Oh—oh!"

"Why, what's the matter?" asked Fairy Lady and Scissors Shears in one breath.

"Why,—they're gone! They're gone! They're gone—the trunk is empty! Who could have stolen them? Ou—ou—! Ou! Ou!"

"They're gone!" sobbed Scissors Shears.

"They're gone!" cried Emery Bag.

"They've went!" said Tommy Pin Cushion.

[254]

"They're gone!" cried Emery Bag

"What—shall—I—do? What—shall—I—do? What shall—I—do?" sobbed Mary Frances.

"What was in there?" asked Fairy Lady.

"Oh, that sweet little kimono and Mary Marie's bath robe, and—her—her—everything—they were all in the trunk. Last night, when I finished her tippet, I put that in. I'm sure I did! I wanted to show them all to Mother, and now, I won't have them. Oh, dear! Mary Marie has on her nightie—that's all that's left of her lovely, lovely things!"

"Perhaps you didn't put them in the trunk," suggested Scissors Shears; "one can be mistaken about such things."

"I feel certain—sure," said Mary Frances, "but I'll go look in my room again."

.   .   .   .   .

"I'm so sorry," said Fairy Lady, "I didn't think she'd mind so. We don't want to hurt her feelings."

"What shall we do?" asked Scissors Shears. "We don't dare tell her until the last lesson—the King said—"

As Mary Frances neared the door she heard voices;

"What shall we do?"

"I feel certain — sure"

but when she stepped in, all was still.   She was crying as hard as ever.

"No," she sobbed, "they're not there!   They are all gone!"

Then suddenly remembering how everyone had stopped talking, she began to be curious.

"Why!" she said, "can it be possible that you know anything about them?"

They all looked guilty and waited for Fairy Lady to answer.

"Listen, little Lady Seamstress," said Fairy Lady, "you will find them all again!"

Mary Frances began to dry her tears.

"Will I?   Will I, dear, dear Fairy Lady?   Why,—how?   They are not gone forever?"

"No," smiled Fairy Lady, "they are not—they are yours; and we will help you find them.   We don't quite know where they are now;   but if—

"Will I, dear, dear Fairy Lady?"

"Little Marie has lost her clothes,
    And can't tell where to find them;
Let them alone, and they'll come home,
    With all their buttons behind them."

"You will find them all again!"

"Oh, thank you, my dear friends,—when will that be?" cried Mary Frances, brightening up.

"Not until to-morrow. Come early if you can— we think we will get word from the Thimble King to-morrow; but we must wait."

"Is it a secret? Oh, I'm so relieved!" said Mary Frances, "and Mary Marie will be all right in this warm weather in only her nightie;—but I can borrow one of Angie's dresses! I forgot!—I'll go put it on her."

What—shall—I—do? What— shall—I—do?"

Chapter XXXIII

Mary Frances visits Thimble Land

"TO-DAY I am to know all about where your dresses went, my dear Mary Marie, and I'm so excited I can hardly wait," said Mary Frances, hugging the dolly close to her as she went into the sewing room.

Sewing Bird did not look up at her, nor seem to notice what she said.

"I wonder why Sewing Bird doesn't glance at me," she thought. "Dear little bird, she may be tired. I'm tired, too, really! Hu—hm," she yawned, and leaned back in her chair, holding her arms closely about Mary Marie. "I believe I'll just shut my eyes and wait for Sewing Bird to 'come to.'"

Everything was quiet for a while, then suddenly a voice—the voice of Sewing Bird—

"I am so excited!"

"She's just in time!
A minute more—

[258]

She never could
Get in the door!"

Mary Frances looked at Sewing Bird.

"How do you do, Sewing Bird, dear," she said.

"Come," said Sewing Bird, "we must hurry. Come!"

"We're here!" laughed Mary Frances. "Why 'hurry,' or why 'come'?"

"Don't spend time talking," exclaimed Sewing Bird rather impatiently.

Mary Frances remembered it was the first time she had ever spoken other than most gently to her.

"If you do, you may think we're there now."

"Don't you want to go?"

"Why, she must be crazy," thought Mary Frances. "What a way to talk!"

"No," she said aloud, "I think we're here now— but when we're there, we're—

"Don't you want to go?" asked Sewing Bird.

"Of course!" said Mary Frances, although she'd no notion where.

"Well, that's good," said the little bird.

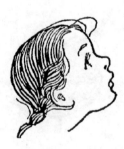

"Of course!" said Mary Frances

"Good!" said Scissors Shears.

"Let us be off," said Sewing Bird.

"Off!" said Scissors Shears.

"Sounds as though we were off," said Mary Frances.

"Not yet," said Sewing Bird. "Here!" And she jumped up and pecked Mary Frances between her shoulders.

The little girl had the strangest sensation. She suddenly felt as light as air,—as though her body weighed nothing. Her nose felt strange, and she thought she ought to find her handkerchief.

"It was in my pocket, I am sure," she said, and started to find her pocket. Imagine her surprise when she couldn't find her hand.

"Why, where can it be?" she thought. "I'll see if I can move my arm!"

She raised one arm, and then the other, and away she flew. Out the window—and across the blue sky— she, nearly as blue as the sky itself, if she had known it.

"How lovely!" she tried to say aloud, but what she heard herself singing was:

Away she flew

"To float away,
      Far, far away,
      In clouds of blue
      And every hue—
      I flit my wing
      And sing and sing!"

Then came another voice:

"I'm so glad, dear little friend,
      My trouble now is at an end;
      'Twas indeed my task of love
      To turn you to a burnished dove."

She looked around, and there was Sewing Bird flying beside her, and another tiny little blue bird, keeping close to Sewing Bird.

"What a dear little
      Bird of blue!
      Is she, dear friend,
      A friend of you?"

she asked.

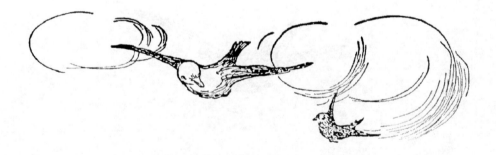

"What a dear little

"A friend she is
    Indeed of me—
    But more of you—
    It's Miss Marie!"

answered Sewing Bird.

"My dear sweet dolly,
    I declare!
    She makes a beauteous bird—
    And rare!"

sang Mary Frances.

"Now, turn again
    To the right wing—
    To Thimble Land
    We safely bring,"

sang Sewing Bird. And Mary Frances, the Dove; and Mary Marie, the Blue Bird; and Sewing Bird Fairy Lady stood before a golden gate.

"You'll have to become a Thimble Person to enter,"

smiled Fairy Lady, and she touched Mary Frances'
right wing with her bodkin wand; and Mary Frances
felt herself stiffen and stiffen.

"What am I now, please?" she asked Fairy Lady.

"You're a Work Basket," said Fairy Lady.

"How curious it feels," said Mary Frances.   "And
Mary Marie—what is she?" she asked.

"She's Bees Wax," whispered Fairy Lady.

"Who's there?" came a voice at the gate, and
before Mary Frances could look for Mary Marie,
"The pass-word?" came the same voice.

"P. P. B. S.," answered Fairy Lady.

"What's that mean, please?" asked Mary
Frances.

"Patience and Perseverance — Bring — Success,"
answered Fairy Lady.

"She's Bees Wax"

"Enter," said Big Thimble, opening the gates,
and Mary Frances and Mary Marie, and Fairy Lady
walked in.

Everybody was there!   Scissors Shears, Silver
Thimble, Pen Cil, Needle Book, and all the others.

My! they were delighted to see them, and gathered about, asking all kinds of questions.

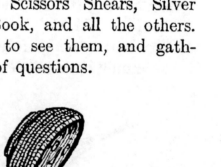

"You're a Work Basket"

"How does it seem to be a basket?" asked Scissors Shears.

"I feel just a little wooden," said Mary Frances, "and rather too large around for my arms,—but very contented."

"Oh, Bees Wax," laughed Tommy Pin Cushion, talking to Mary Marie, "you always had a waxen look to me."

"It is lovely to be able to speak," said Bees Wax, otherwise Mary Marie. "I would like to thank Mamma, and you all—"

"Here comes His Majesty!" exclaimed Scissors Shears. Everybody bowed toward the ground except Fairy Lady, and Mary Frances Work Basket, and Mary Marie Bees Wax.

Mary Frances looked up.

Coming between two huckleberry bushes (trees, Mary Frances thought them) was an airship made of golden basketry. Gracefully down it floated, with a little zdud! zdud! sound, and in it sat—Mary Frances knew him in a minute—the King of Fairy Thimble Land!

His coat was of green and gold, but it was so glossy

t's lovely
o be
ible to
speak"

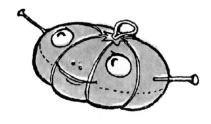

"Oh, Bees Wax" laughed Tommy Pin Cushion

Mary Frances was herself
again—but a very tiny self

and fine that Mary Frances thought it was spun of cobwebs.   He held a long golden needle in his hand.

"Where are they?" he asked.

"Your Majesty," said Fairy Lady, "here they are!"

"Oh," said the King of Thimble Land to Mary Frances Work Basket, and Mary Marie Bees Wax. "Step up and bow!"

Mary Frances tried to kneel, thinking this w s proper, but the King touched her with his wand; then he touched Bees Wax.

Mary Frances was herself again—but a very tiny self—not so large as Sewing Bird Fairy Lady,—and beside her was a little girl with golden curls, just half as tall as Fairy Lady.

"Mother!" said the tiny little thing, smiling to Mary Frances.

"Attention!" roared the King of Thimble Land.

"Attention!" roared the King

"I beg your Majesty's pardon," said Mary Frances, "but she's never spoken to me before—and"—

"That will do," said the King. "If a doll is more important than I,—sew her up!"

"In what, Your Majesty?" asked Bod Kin.

"Oh, no, no!" exclaimed Mary Frances. "I didn't mean it that way!"

"You better not!" said the King. "But I understand,"—he added, seeing Mary Frances look sad. "You must know I understand how you feel,

"When you see
All her lost dresses,
On this tree,"

I didn't
mean it
that way!

and he pointed to a little tree nearby. There were all Mary Marie's pretty lost clothes!

"You may take them with you," said the King, smiling.

"Never in all the years of Thimble History," he went on, "have we been so interested in any little girl. I borrowed these to show some other little girls what patience and perseverance will do.

"Now, I am going to bestow on you one of my loveliest gifts; for I saw all your beautiful work, and the Grand Sampler! A prize indeed, you shall have! From to-day, the Needle-of-Don't-Have-to-Try is yours— to keep! We give one something like it to all good

"You may take them with you"

girls who try to do their best, but yours is the Fairy Needle-of-Don't-Have-to-Try.

"And one more surprise! You may tell your mother about us, and explain about the dolly's clothes. Please pack them all, attendants!"

"Here's the suit case!" said Fairy Lady, handing out Mary Marie's little suit case, "and over there is the trunk. Put the caps in the tray, remember!"

"You have saved us from being Never-Nevers," continued the King, "because you kept the secret until you finished the lessons. And now, that you are going—here is a bag of useful gifts for you to open when you reach home. Pack the bag in the suit case, attendants."

"We'd love to keep you longer"

"We'd love to keep you longer—you, and sweet Mary Marie—but your Grandma has called you twice. You may show her all the pretty things you've made, when you get home. Let us know when you want us again, unless you wish" (and the King laughed) "to say forever—Good-bye. Who'll say Good-bye forever?" he asked.

"Oh, Your Majesty, not I!" said Mary Frances.

"Not I!" answered every one of the Thimble People.

.   .   .   .   .   .

Mary Frances opened her eyes. Did Sewing Bird or Dick Canary sing,

"Not I!"

Out the window—and across the blue sky

CHAPTER XXXIV

WHAT WAS IN THE FAIRY BAG

THESE are the things Mary Frances found in the bag in Mary Marie's suit case when she got home:

Rain
Coat

PATTERN 27.—DOLL'S RAIN COAT

See Insert V

NOTE.—Make rain coat about an inch longer than cape.
To cut out—
1. Cut out by pattern of Fur-lined Cape.
In the fronts, cut open the Arm Flap Opening.
Do not cut a collar.
2. Cut hood, having arrow edge (⟫→) of pattern on lengthwise fold of goods.
3. Cut four arm flaps.
To make—
1. Make in same way as Fur-lined Cape, but without a lining. Press seams open.
2. *Before joining shoulder seams,* face fronts back as in making. Automobile Coat.
3. Pin two arm flaps together, right sides facing.

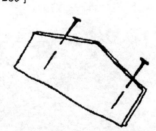

Stitch one-eighth inch from all edges except the arrow edge (➤➤➤➤). Turn inside out.

Baste along the stitched edges.

Stitch along the basted edges.

4. Sew to flap-opening in position shown by dotted lines on pattern.

As in putting on a band, stitch first through a single thickness of open edge of flap. Turn; baste and hem down other edge.

5. Overhand closely and blanket-stitch the under edge of flap opening.

6. Make a very narrow hem around the circular edge of hood, or line with plaid silk.

7. Three-quarter inch from edge of hood (see dotted line on pattern) run a gathering thread of very coarse cotton. Do not draw up the gathers.

8. Make a three-quarter inch hem in bottom of coat.

9. Matching double notches carefully, pin the hood to the coat, with wrong sides facing each other.

Join hood to coat with French seam.

10. Try coat on doll. Draw up and fasten the gathers of hood to fit head.

Draw up gathers to fit head

PATTERN 28.—DOLL'S POLO CAP

See Insert VIII

To cut—

(Material: white corduroy.)

1. Cut four pieces like pattern of Polo Cap.

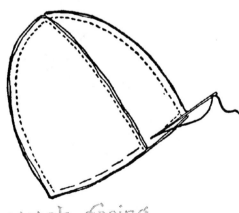

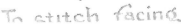
To stitch facing.

2. Cut a bias strip of goods, two and one-half inches wide, twelve and one-half inches long.

To make—

1. Beginning at the point, baste sections of cap together, right sides facing each other.

Match the notches.

Stitch each seam.

2. Join ends of bias strip or band, in a plain seam.

3. Turn in one edge of band one-quarter inch.

4. Turn cap wrong side out.

Baste other edge of band to the edge of cap, having the right sides of band and cap facing.

In doing this work, stretch edge of bias band a little.

5. Stitch one-quarter inch from edge.

6. Turn band or facing up on wrong side.

Baste and hem in place.

(See dotted line on pattern.)

7. Turn cap right side out.

Turn up faced edge of cap on outside, nearly the full width.

PATTERN 29.—DOLL'S WEDDING DRESS

NOTE.—Cut and make a guimpe of lace.   (Pattern 19.)

Do not use bands for sleeves, but cut sleeves narrower than pattern, and place the scalloped edge of lace at ends of sleeves.

Scalloped edge of lace for sleeves

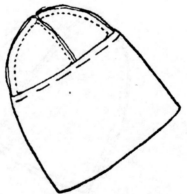

Turn facing up on wrong side

To Cut Wedding Dress

See Insert X

1. Spread goods out on table.

2. Pin pattern for Front of Wedding Dress with arrow on lengthwise of goods.

3. Pin pattern for Back of Wedding Dress on goods.

Place the shoulders of both patterns together. Cut out. (See picture.)

4. Prick, with a pin, through lines showing the plaits, or use a tracing wheel. Remove pattern, and run basting thread through these pinholes.

Cut a separate train,—for lining of the train of wedding dress. Cut it like the pattern of the train.

To make—

1. Baste lining train-section to train of dress, right sides facing.

Stitch one-quarter inch from edge. **Turn, and** baste along edges.

2. To Make Plaits—

Fold goods backward along the lines of basting nearest the center-front and center-back. Baste.

Bring folded edge over to other line of basting.

3. Lay flat, and baste all the way to bottom of dress and train. Press with a warm iron.

4. Stitch plaits down four inches from the waist line in front, and three inches in back.

Bring folded edge over to basting

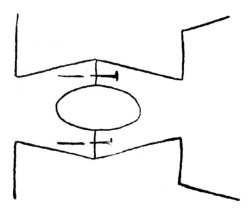

Pin shoulders together

5. Finish neck with a very narrow hem.   Work French knots around the hem.

6. Make a narrow hem from waist line in front, across the shoulders, to waist line in back.

7. Join skirt with French seams.

8. Face the skirt, under arms, with an inch-wide bias facing.

9. Open plaits at bottom of dress.

10. Cut a bias facing one and one-quarter inches wide, for bottom of dress.   Baste facing on right side.   Stitch one-quarter inch from edge.   Turn up on wrong side.

Baste.   Turn in, and hem the facing on wrong side.

11.   Turn in and hem the facing of train.

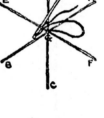

Spider's
Web

PATTERN 30.—LADIES' WORK BAG

Cut bag ten inches wide, and twenty-eight inches long. Make like Laundry Bag.   Do not overhand seams, but make French seams.

Or,

Use a large flowered handkerchief.

1. Fold handkerchief through the center, wrong side out.

2. Stitch through the center of the folded handkerchief.

3. Fold over on the stitching.

4. Stitch, or overhand the two folded edges which are lying together.

5. On one side of handkerchief turn down one thickness of goods.   (Like an envelope flap.)

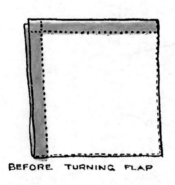

BEFORE TURNING FLAP

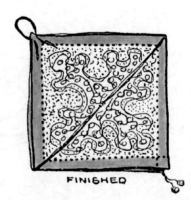

FINISHED

Ladies' Work Bag

Do the same to the other side. "Tack" the center of the upper part of the folded edge of the flap to the *single* thickness lying just beneath. Do same to other side.

6. Make a small "box" plait (or double plait) in each single thickness of handkerchief at top.

7. Sew the plaits together, and fasten a loop between the plaits.

Finish bag with two little cotton balls, sewed to the lowest point.

This makes a many-pocketed bag, and would be a pleasing Christmas gift to your mother.

PATTERN 31.—LADIES' BELT

1. Buy belting which is sold by the running yard.

2. Embroider the design given on this page upon the belt.

Trace design through carbon paper; or transfer by tracing through tissue page, and turning the picture face-down on the material; trace picture again on wrong side.

PATTERN 32.—BABIES' BIB

1. Buy smallest size "huck-a-back" towel.

2. Embroider on it the cross-stitch design given on this page.

3. Through tracing paper, copy outline of neck given on this page. Cut out pattern.

4. Fold towel through center lengthwise.

Cut neck by pattern.

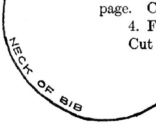

Ladies belt design

NECK OF BIB

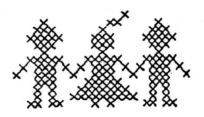

Cross stitch pattern

29. Wedding Dress

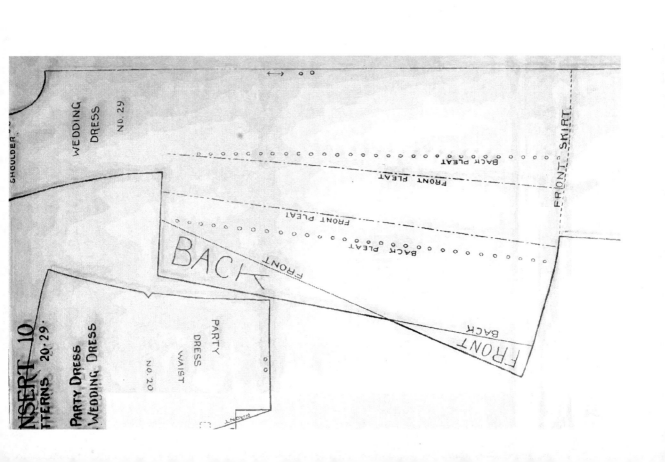

INSERT 10
PATTERNS 20·29·

PARTY DRESS
WEDDING DRESS

PARTY
DRESS

WAIST

NO. 20

WEDDING
DRESS

NO. 29

SHOULDER

BACK

FRONT

FRONT PLEAT

BACK PLEAT

FRONT PLEAT

BACK PLEAT

FRONT SKIRT

FRONT
BACK

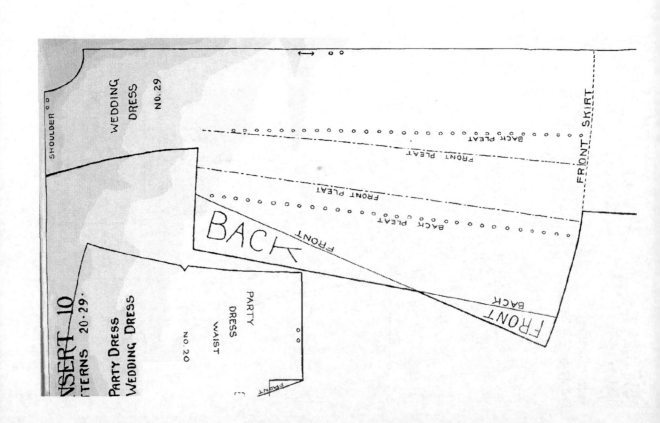

5. Bind neck with cotton or linen tape, leaving ends long enough to tie.

PATTERN 33.—GIRLS' COLLAR

1. Trace pattern of collar through tissue or transfer paper. Cut out.

2. Place pattern with double ring (oo) edge on a lengthwise fold of linen.

3. Trace design on collar.

4. Embroider scallops with close blanket stitches.

5. Embroider rings with close "over-and-under" stitches— Satin Stitch.

41.—FRENCH HEMMING ON DAMASK

For folding table linen or damask, fold and crease a very narrow hem, then fold the hem back on the right side, and over-hand the edge thus folded.   Press open on right side.

NOTE.—Or, run through the hemmer of the sewing machine, having the needle unthreaded, using a very fine stitch: proceed as above.

42.—DARNING STOCKINGS

1. In learning to darn, it is well to use a piece of flexible card board, three and one-half inches long by three inches wide.

2. With a large needle, puncture it three-quarters of an inch from the top, and three-quarters of an inch from the bottom, making holes one-eighth of an inch apart.

Girls' Collar pattern

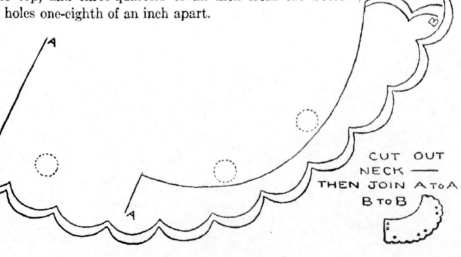

CUT OUT NECK —— THEN JOIN A TO A B TO B

3. Use zephyr, in a tapestry needle, and work as in picture on this page.

4. Weave, with a contrasting shade of zephyr, in and out of the long stitches already taken.

Cut a hole in a piece of muslin: draw edge together with the fingers, and darn with cotton thread as above. Stockings are darned in the same way. In actual darning never use a knot.

43.—DARNING WOOLEN GOODS

Darning is usually done by use of the running stitch. Use fine thread—cotton is preferred, about the size of the weaving threads of the goods. Draw the edges of the tear together, and weave across the opening with the running stitch. If the tear is very large, first baste a piece of goods like the garment under the tear, and take the stitches into this. Sometimes a raveling thread of the material is used to make an almost invisible darn.

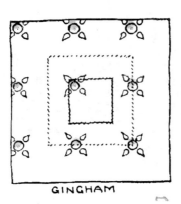

Darning Stitch

44.—PATCHING ON GINGHAM

1. Cut the hole to make a small square, clip corners, turn edges back and baste.

2. Cut piece of goods three-quarters of an inch larger, on each side, than the hole thus formed, being careful to match figures of material. Clip corners off this piece and turn goods back on right side one-quarter of an inch, and crease.

3. Pin and baste this under the hole, matching figures carefully, and hem down, on right side and wrong side. Remove bastings.

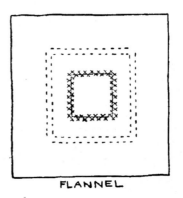

GINGHAM   FLANNEL

NOTE.—Or a piece of goods may be cut one-quarter of an inch larger than the hole on each side and edges turned back one-quarter of an inch. Overhand each edge of the patch to each edge of the hole.

45.—PATCHING ON FLANNEL

This is done in the same way as the hemmed patch on gingham, except that the edges are not turned in, but are catch-stitched down on both right and wrong side, as shown in picture.

46.—SPIDER'S WEB

An ornamental lace stitch.

Use a piece of muslin three inches by six inches for practice.

1. Fold it and baste edges. Thread a large needle with the red cotton, as used in former lessons.

Draw or trace a figure like drawing shown on page 273.

2. From underside of muslin, enter needle at *a*; pull through; point downward at *b*, upward at *c*, downward at *d*, upward at *e*, downward at *f*.

3. On wrong side, bring needle to the center *g*, at the crossing of the long stitches, and pull through to right side.

4. Holding muslin in left hand, point the threaded eye of the needle toward you, under the thread *ge*; pull through; under *gd*, and *ga*, under *gf*, and continue until web is formed. Fasten in usual manner.

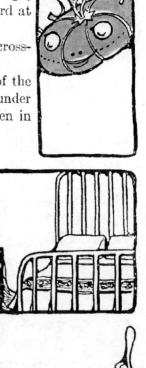

Doll's Wedding Dress

CHAPTER XXXV

MARY FRANCES AT HOME

MARY FRANCES came into her mother's room on the evening of the day they all reached home.

"Oh, Mother, I have the loveliest surprise for you! Please shut your eyes and don't peep. It will take me some time to get it ready."

"Yes, dear," smiled her mother, "but I'm very anxious to see!"

Mary Frances unlocked Mary Marie's trunk, and spread all the contents out on the bed.

"Oh, Mother I have the loveliest surprise for you!"

"I'll be back in one minute. Don't you peep, Mother, dear!" she begged as she ran out of the room.

She brought back Mary Marie, dressed in her party dress and summer hat, and sat her up on the pillow.

"Now," she cried, kissing her mother, "now, you may look, Mother, dear!"

"Why, what in the world, my dear little girl? Where did all these lovely clothes come from?"

"Why, what in the world, my dear little girl?"

She spends hours in the sewing room".

JANE A. BOYER

"I made them, Mother,—I mean—I, and the Thimble People."

"You made them!" exclaimed her mother; "not that lovely kimono and bath robe, and those cunning little bonnets, and that lovely automobile coat!"

"Every one!" cried Mary Frances, dancing up and down.

"Why, dear," said her mother, "I cannot believe my eyes! I thought you did very, very well in the few sewing lessons by mail, but I never dreamed—"

"If the Thimble People hadn't helped me, Mother, I never could have made them; and if you hadn't sent me the beautiful goods, and my dear, lovely dolly, I couldn't have done it! It had to be a secret until I finished the lessons—I couldn't tell Grandma,— and I was crazy to tell you!"

Showed bundle of patterns

"Who are the Thimble People?" asked her mother. Then Mary Frances told all about her new friends.

When she finished, she showed the bundle of patterns last given her by the Thimble King.

"We'll make these together, Mother, dear—if you say so?"

"I certainly do say so, dear," said her mother.

"Who are the Thimble People?"

"I would like to take some lessons myself—such delightful lessons; will you teach me?"

"I'll do my best,—and—I just believe the Thimble People will help!" said Mary Frances wisely;— and she thought she surely saw Scissors Shears wink at her.

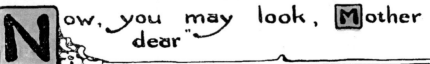

Now, you may look, Mother dear"

Lightning Source UK Ltd.
Milton Keynes UK
UKOW022321060113

204492UK00004B/269/P